Invisible Wealth

Invisible Wealth

5 Principles for Redefining Personal Wealth in the New Paradigm

Jennifer Wines

WILEY

Published by John Wiley & Sons, Inc., Hoboken, New Jersey.
Published simultaneously in Canada.

For general information on our other products and services or for technical support, please contact our Customer Care Department within the United States at (800) 762-2974, outside the United States at (317) 572-3993 or fax (317) 572-4002.

Wiley also publishes its books in a variety of electronic formats. Some content that appears in print may not be available in electronic formats. For more information about Wiley products, visit our web site at www.wiley.com.

Library of Congress Cataloging-in-Publication Data:

Names: Wines, Jennifer, author.
Title: Invisible wealth : 5 principles for the new wealth paradigm /
  Jennifer Wines.
Description: Hoboken, New Jersey : John Wiley & Sons, Inc., [2023] |
  Includes index.
Identifiers: LCCN 2022052837 (print) | LCCN 2022052838 (ebook) | ISBN
  9781394180530 (hardback) | ISBN 9781394180554 (adobe pdf) | ISBN
  9781394180547 (epub)
Subjects: LCSH: Wealth. | Interpersonal relations.
Classification: LCC HB251 .W564 2023 (print) | LCC HB251 (ebook) | DDC
  330.1/6—dc23/eng/20230119
LC record available at https://lccn.loc.gov/2022052837
LC ebook record available at https://lccn.loc.gov/2022052838

Cover Design: Wiley
Cover Image: © Micha Frank/Unsplash

SKY10044704_032223

For my granny, who always wanted to write a book.
And for my mom, who inspired me to write one.
We are forever three leaves of the
same shamrock.

Contents

Preface

Conversations were shifting, with my private wealth management clients, with my friends, and within myself. These shifts in conversations were, and remain, emblematic of the paradigm shifts currently underway in our society. There's an undercurrent of change happening, which is revealing itself through conversation and constructive action. We, individually and collectively, are revisiting values (qualitative) and value (quantitative) within our (economic) ecosystems; thereby, revisiting our concept of wealth. After all, value and wealth are inextricably linked.

And as it so happens, wealth is something I'm quite familiar with, after working in the world of private wealth management for over a decade—although, in April 2022, I left a great company, a great team, and great clients in order to fully commit myself to (what I term) the *new wealth paradigm*. These shifts in conversations and paradigms propelled me into researching well-established axioms and maxims of wealth, long before leaving my job. In fact, in retrospect, it feels as though my whole life was designed to place me in a position for writing *Invisible Wealth*. Law school included, which is where I fell in love with the written word.

Language is the oldest technology in the book. And while technological advancements have much to do with the paradigm shifts we're experiencing, it's words that enable us to communicate thoughts, ideas, and narratives relating to such advancements. What's more, these narratives—or collective conversations—help us to exchange ideas with one another, in order to flush out and define (or perhaps redefine) concepts and, by extension, applications of those concepts. Words are powerful. With this backdrop in mind, it's my hope that these architected ideas are helpful to you—for revisiting, and perhaps redefining, your concept of wealth—*what's your wealth*?

Part I

When I was growing up, my grandmother had a watercolor painting hanging on the bathroom wall; it was a painting of a personified frog who was relaxing in a bubble bath while holding a glass of champagne; the painting read: *you can never be too rich or too thin.* The message was clear: the more money, the better; the skinnier, the better. While the painting was playful and funny, there's no denying that it played back a set of values that permeate(d) society.

I'm an immigrant and the first person in my family to attend college in the United States. Like many other millennials, I started my adult life burdened with six figures of student loan debt, starting life at a financial deficit. After graduating from undergrad and law school, I entered the world of finance. And while my profession as a wealth management advisor has provided an intimate lens into the world of the super wealthy, I've also personally experienced wealth, in every sense of the word. My life has provided insight into both ends of the financial wealth spectrum. There were times when I would watch my single mom put $3.11 worth of gas into the car just to make it to and from work (ahead of the next paycheck). There was also a time when I vacationed in the South of France on a 311-foot superyacht.

Through a myriad of experiences, both personally and professionally, I've observed, learned, and researched valuable lessons regarding wealth—within the context of our rapidly evolving world.

We are in the midst of a huge paradigm shift, rethinking what we value and therefore rethinking how we define wealth. This shift caught exponential wind during the past couple of years when our lives turned inside out (or was it outside in?), as we turned inward and reflected. The pandemic invited us to rethink, rediscover, and reinvent ourselves. We upgraded our own internal software, all the while upgrading our Zoom software. And Zoom we did, both inwards and outwards. These upgrades ushered in reinvention of self, extending to the rise of the personal brand, which now competes with the company brand. At the same time, we are seeing significant advancements in technology, thus bolstering our digital world alongside the "real" world. Toss in blockchain technology, the Great Resignation, and the fact that the entrepreneurial spirit animals are alive and well, and we have ourselves a dynamic environment. We're currently playing what feels like four-dimensional chess.

Given this confluence of circumstances, we now have a ripe opportunity to reimagine and redefine wealth, because so much of what we value, both individually and collectively, is shifting. The way we make, invest, transact, and spend money is changing right before our eyes. We are witnessing the move from corporate cubicles to the creator economy, from dollar bills to digital dollars, and from the purchasing of things to the purchasing of experiences. As a society, we are becoming increasingly comfortable with pegging value to intangible assets, as we fundamentally always have. To put it neatly, we are shifting into a world that values intangibles over the tangibles: *Invisible Wealth*.

Chapter 1
Defining and Redefining Wealth

We are shifting into a *new wealth paradigm* that's inviting us to reimagine and redefine our definition and concept of wealth. The antiquated wealth narrative typically equates wealth to an abundance of money; we're wealthy when we have lots of money. We see this messaging everywhere, watercolor frog paintings included. And while there is an interconnected relationship between wealth and money, now is the time to revisit the premise that they are merely one and the same. But before we can *redefine* wealth, we must first *define* it. Additionally, by exploring the concept of wealth, we'll explore the relationship between wealth, money, and the economy. First, we'll take a look at how these three concepts are braided together; thereafter, we'll untie the braid and focus on each thread independently: What is wealth? What is money? and What is an economy?

The Relationship Between Wealth, Money, and the Economy

We're familiar with the idea that wealth equates to an abundance of money. The intertwined relationship between wealth and money has a lot to do with the advancements in our economies; the more efficient economies became, the more synonymous wealth and money became. An economy is

3

a system where goods and services are produced, sold, and bought, within a country or region.[1] The introduction and use of money within economies allowed economies to scale, thereby increasing the potential for (financial) wealth creation. Throughout this chapter, we'll unpack how and why economies became more advanced and efficient over time, thereby influencing the intertwined relationship between wealth and money.

What Is Wealth?

Let's start with a simple question: *What is wealth?*

Take a moment to answer this for yourself.

What came to mind?

Odds are, your mind went to one of two places: either that wealth is having lots of money, or a forced pause and ponder. Regardless of which fork in the (mental) road you went down, each response invites a deeper look into what *wealth* is.

First Principles Thinking

The best way to approach the question *What is wealth?* is through a critical thinking model called first principles thinking. This turn of phrase has gotten a lot of attention lately thanks to the likes of Elon Musk. Despite the recent attention of this phrase, first principles thinking has been around since the days of Aristotle, around 350 BC. Therefore, it is a tried-and-true methodology. This critical thinking model requires the breaking down of a concept, idea, or problem into its most fundamental parts. Per Aristotle, first principles thinking is "the first basis from which a thing is known."[2] Per Elon Musk, "First principles is a physics way of looking at the world. You boil things down to the most fundamental truths and then reason up from there."[3]

From that, we can extrapolate that if we want to understand what *wealth* is, by definition, then a great place to start is with where the word came from—its etymology. Etymology is the study of the origin of a word, and how the meaning of a word changes over time. In other words, we are looking at the genesis of the word *wealth*. We can more fully appreciate the word *wealth* by understanding where the first basis (or instance) of the word was used (first principles). From there, we can explore how the meaning has changed over time, and the reasons for this evolutionary change. First principles thinking allows us to break down *wealth* into basic, etymological building blocks, to then reassemble it's meaning from the bottom up, within the context of today's world.

The Etymology of Wealth

Using the Online Etymology Dictionary, let's take a look at the origins of "wealth" as a noun:

> Mid 13-c., "happiness," also "prosperity in abundance of possessions or riches," from Middle English wele "well-being" (see weal (n.1)) on analogy of health.[4]

Given the definition suggests we look at "weal," let's go ahead and do so here:

> "well-being," Old English wela "wealth," in late Old English also "welfare, well-being," from West Germanic *welon-, from PIE root *wel- (2) "to wish, will" (see will (v)). Related to well (adv.)[5]

Next, here's what the etymology dictionary provides for the adjective "wealthy."

> Late 14-c., "happy, prosperous," from wealth + -y (2). Meaning "rich, opulent" is from early 15-c. Noun meaning "wealthy persons collectively" is from late 14-c.[6]

Finally, here's a look at the etymology of "commonweal," given that we just saw a nod to collective wealth:

> Mid 14-c., comen wele, "a commonwealth or its people;" mid-15c., comune wele, "the public good, the general welfare of a nation or community;" see common (adj.) + weal (n.1).[7]

Now let's string these etymological pearls of insight together. First things first, the word *wealth* came into our lexicon in the mid-thirteenth century, compliments of England; *wealthy* came next, followed by *commonwealth*. It's fascinating that wealth started out as a noun relating to the individual and then wealthy came into our lexicon as an adjective to describe an individual. Finally, the term expanded conceptual reach to that of the community in the mid-fifteenth century. Following this logic, we can deduce that wealth related to the individual first, and then to society as a whole second. This logic supports the premise that wealth originally started as an individualistic construct: personal wealth, thereby supporting community wealth.

Furthermore, the word *wealth* initially took on a more expansive definition in the mid-thirteenth century. Originally, wealth expanded into the realms of possessions, happiness, health, and well-being. It embodied a wider array of concepts, covering both the tangible and intangible aspects of wealth—a multidimensional definition; a totality of being. What's interesting is that the fundamental roots of the word related to health and well-being, more so than anything else. Over time, the definition and concept of wealth narrowed to our current wealth narrative, which suggests that wealth relates to money and material wealth, generally speaking.[8] This is the antiquated wealth paradigm. This reflects the fact that over time—from the thirteenth century up through today—the relationship between wealth and money evolved, ultimately becoming tightly intertwined, nearly collapsing into one and the same.

This then begs the question: *What is money?*

> *"What can be added to the happiness of a man who is in health, out of debt, and has a clear conscience?"*
>
> —*Adam Smith*

What Is Money?

Money used to be a crisp (or not) green piece of paper we'd line our wallets with. Maybe you'd fold a $10 bill into a secret compartment within your wallet as a kid—for a rainy day. I remember having a multicolored, neon wallet with Velcro compartments, which I loved. I also remember the sound and feel of peeling the Velcro panels apart, granting access to my hard-earned money—money I earned from my after-school, 3.5-hour shift at Filene's department store in New Hampshire. My then-boyfriend would drive me

30 minutes to and from work, where I made less than $10 an hour, all to line my favorite neon wallet with.

Money is a tool used to transfer value within an economy, because it is an expression of value. Money has specific attributes that enable it to work within an economy. The functional attributes of money unlock the potential for an increasingly efficient economy. So long as these attributes (listed later) are satisfied, the monetary tool of popular choice can be used to transfer value across society. Consider this historical example: there was a time when cowry shells were considered money. Some of you may be scratching your head thinking, shells, really? And yes, it turns out cowry shells do embody the attributes necessary to function as money. Here are the three primary functions of money, plus the use case for cowry shells, in parallel:

1. *Store of Value:* Money can be saved and used later because it retains its value over time—in perpetuity. Money retains its value over time because of its durable nature—meaning it doesn't rot, rust, or decay (which would otherwise diminish its value). Money also exists in finite supply (scarcity), preserving the integrity of its value.

   Cowry shells retain their value over time because they are durable. In other words, cowry shells don't rot, rust, or decay. There is also a finite supply of cowry shells in the world.

2. *Unit of Account:* Money must exist in small, standardized units for less valuable exchanges and aggregated together for more valuable exchanges. The units of account must be divisible, fungible, and measurable.

   Cowry shells are standardized units that are divisible, fungible, and measurable, because of their consistently small size and shape. Each cowry shell can easily represent one unit of value, and can be aggregated together for more valuable exchanges.

3. *Medium of Exchange:* Money can be used to buy and sell from one another, facilitating exchange. This is possible when money is portable (easy to transport or transmit), and when the monetary tool is widely accepted by society.

Cowry shells can be used to buy and sell from one another, facilitating exchange. This is possible because they are easy to transport, and were a widely accepted monetary tool within society.

With this backdrop in mind, we see how cowry shells used to be used as money. Initially, natural objects were the natural, go-to option as money. Over time, the sophistication of money evolved and so did our economies.

So how did cowry shells evolve into the next form of money? Categorically, the evolutionary timeline of money looks like this: commodity money, representative money, fiat money, and electronic/digital money. We are seeing a clear shift from tangible, visible currency to intangible, *invisible* currency. Let's dive in.

> *"All money is a matter of belief."*
>
> —*Adam Smith*

Commodity Money

First up is *commodity money*. Commodity money has intrinsic value independent of its value as money. Take gold, for example. Gold has intrinsic value and also satisfies all the functions and characteristics of money detailed earlier. Therefore, this esteemed metal became an attractive—pun intended—tool for economic exchange. Gold's strong yet malleable nature makes it perfect for coin creation, which is exactly what the Kingdom of Lydia (current day Turkey) decided to do around 600 BCE. Lydia was the first empire to issue regulated coins. These coins were considered regulated because the government authority issued them. You could see that the coins were issued by a government authority because the coins had certified markings on them to signify they were intended as a specific value of exchange.[9] From 600 BCE onward, gold has maintained its stronghold in societies and economies.

Despite gold maintaining its stronghold, the vulnerabilities of gold as money started to reveal themselves—especially as societies, economies, and greed grew. The biggest example of these vulnerabilities relate to the durability, portability, and counterfeit susceptibility of the metal. Gold has high durability given its high density and noncorrosive properties, but gold coins can still be tampered with. Someone can shave a little gold off a coin or bullion bar—a little off the top and into their pocket. Or someone might dilute the gold with another (less valuable) metal prior to minting. Moving beyond the durability and counterfeit susceptibilities, large amounts of gold are hard to move around. Because of its high density, gold is heavy and not the most conducive for strolling around town with. As societies and economies expanded, gold coins and bars became a less attractive means of exchange. Hence, the next iteration of money.

Representative Money

The next iteration of money is *representative money.* Just like commodity money, the name representative money is pretty intuitive. Representative money is paper money that represents the valuable commodity (asset) it can be exchanged for, like gold. The paper represents the commodity it's backed by, but the paper in and of itself has no value. One brings the representative, paper money to the bank and redeems it for the commodity it represents. This makes representative money akin to a debt instrument: aka an "I owe you." For example, checks are considered representative money. When you bring a check to the bank and "cash it in," you get the money owed in return. These valuable papers were designed to create more trust and practical efficiency in economic trade by way of less counterfeiting lighter pockets. Replacing gold coins for paper money reduced counterfeit susceptibility, and transaction friction. Therefore, paper money increased the efficiency of trade, thereby increasing the sophistication of economies. You're more likely to travel further, geographically, to purchase an expensive item if money is light and portable. Plus, the purchaser is more likely to transact if they can trust the authenticity of the money. Win/win.

At this point in the evolutionary timeline of money, all money was local—meaning the state-chartered banks issued representative money, readily redeemable for gold (or silver). Therefore, trust in the issuing bank was imperative and regulations helped to establish and maintain this trust. Regulations required that a bank maintain enough gold in their vault to back the representative money issued, and in circulation. Otherwise, you ran the risk of holding representative money that represented nothing. In eighteenth- and nineteenth-century America, there were frequent "runs on the bank," which meant people would literally run to the bank to redeem their paper money for gold before the (poorly regulated and untrustworthy) bank ran out.[10]

Clearly, the primary problem with representative money was ensuring that the state-chartered banks would maintain convertibility (from paper to the valuable, underlying commodity). If banks issued or loaned more representative money than they could back with intrinsic value, then this would lead to an expanded money supply, which could create debasement or the devaluing of money. And debasement of money can lead to a systemic collapse of the economic infrastructure.

In comes the federal government.

The federal government (in many countries) recognized the need to regulate the local banks issuing representative money to ensure that the money was in fact backed by intrinsic value, or gold. Therefore, the federal government created policy around money—monetary policy. Initially, this policy was colloquially termed the "gold standard." The gold standard is a monetary system in which a government's paper money is directly linked to gold. In the 1870's, the gold standard became the international standard for valuing currency.[11]

The gold standard was golden . . . until it wasn't. In the United States, President Nixon nixed the gold standard in 1971, ushering in our next category of money, fiat money.[12] This is where things get interesting.

"Gold is money. Everything else is just credit."

—*J.P. Morgan*

Fiat Money

The third iteration of money is *fiat money*. Fiat money, just like commodity and representative money, is pretty literal in its definition when you consider what *fiat* means. Fiat is defined as "an authoritative or arbitrary order" or "an authoritative determination."[13] It follows that fiat money is that which originates by government decree. The money, typically paper money, has no intrinsic value nor does it have representative value. The government that issues the money sets the value of the currency. Fiat money extracts its value from the fact that it is issued and tightly controlled by the government. This is why governments issuing money are hyper focused on two things: making sure the money is not counterfeited and that it is the only standard of money in the economy.

This is a good time to address the relationship between "money" and "currency." Money is an intangible concept, and currency is a tangible representation of the intangible concept of money. Technically, you can't hold money in your hand, but you can hold currency in your hand, which represents the abstraction of money. For example, fiat money is tangibly represented by fiat currency in the form of paper bills and coins.

A government manages the value of its money by controlling how much is in circulation, which is why it's important that currency not be counterfeited. If a third party were to counterfeit fiat money, adding faux currency into the existing supply, this would have negative implications on the supply/demand dynamics of the economy. The economy would experience a devaluation of money, and on the other side of this coin, higher inflation. Note: inflation can also happen when the government, more specifically the central bank, prints additional money for circulation into the economy. We currently have front row seats to this here in the United States, where we saw trillions of dollars added into the economy during the pandemic, ultimately causing inflation to hit as high as 9% (in June 2022).[14,15]

Additionally, a government manages the value of its money by declaring their issued currency legal tender. This decree requires the issued currency be the only acceptable standard of money in use.[16] This means the fiat money issued by the government is the only form of currency recognized for payment of financial obligations, debts, and taxes. Could you imagine if a majority of people decided to use cowry shells to pay for financial obligations instead of legal tender? This would undermine the value of fiat currency because there would be less demand for it. As a result, the supply/demand dynamics would be off-kilter.

Electronic/Digital Money

Electronic/digital money, too, is exactly what it sounds like—electronic/digital money, which exists in a banking computer system, and is available for transaction through electronic systems.[17] Many people consider electronic and digital money to be one and the same, but it's important that we take the time to parse out the distinction between the two. Electronic money moves through electronic systems, and can be turned in for physical, tangible currency. Whereas digital money also moves through electronic systems, but it cannot be turned into physical, tangible currency. Digital currency never takes physical form; it remains on a computer network.[18] Electronic money has the potential for conversion into tangible currency, while digital currency is, and always remains, intangible. This is the distinction.

The intangible nature of electronic/digital money enhances many of the functional attributes of money, hence it's prolific adoption in our increasingly digital world. As a store of value, electronic/digital money is certainly durable because it doesn't rot, rust, or decay; thereby retaining its value in perpetuity. As a unit of account, electronic/digital money can be broken down into small or large standardized units, because it is electronic/digital in nature, existing in a computer system. Finally, electronic/digital money functions as an efficient medium of exchange, because of its portable, easily transmittable (intangible) nature. It is easy to transmit across electronic systems; all you need is your digital wallet (via computer or smartphone) to access your money at any given time. This is why only 10% of the money supply, worldwide, is in physical form.[19] Our predominately cashless society depends upon a strong, technological infrastructure to support economic activity. We've come a long way since my multicolored, neon wallet days.

Bitcoin

There is no literal interpretation for *Bitcoin* like there is for commodity money, representative money, fiat money, and electronic/digital money. Although, consistent with the evolutionary timeline of money, Bitcoin is (purely) digital in nature. Bitcoin was first introduced to the world in 2008 through a white paper titled "Bitcoin: A Peer-to-Peer Electronic Cash System."[20] The title, in and of itself, tells us that the exchange of bitcoin occurs peer-to-peer, which negates the need for an intermediary. The title also tells us that Bitcoin was created for the purpose of being a cash system. Here is the first half of the abstract, which is presented in the white paper:

Abstract. A purely peer-to-peer version of electronic cash would allow online payments to be sent directly from one party to another without going through a financial institution. Digital signatures provide part of the solution, but the main benefits are lost if a trusted third party is still required to prevent double-spending. We propose a solution to the double-spending problem using a peer-to-peer network . . . [21]

Bitcoin has gone (and continues to go) through an identity crises, because of its novel and unique nature. Bitcoin has been socialized as digital money, digital currency (represented by a lower-case b, "bitcoin"), a digital asset, and/or specifically, a digital commodity—depending on who and when you ask.

In August 2022, a new Senate bill emerged, stating that Bitcoin is a commodity; therefore, the Commodity Futures Trading Commission should regulate it.[22] This bill will be voted on in the Senate, before moving to the House (if it's passed). That said, Bitcoin could shape up to be commodity money—digital, commodity money. In other words, Bitcoin could be a multipronged asset, meaning it's both a digital commodity (without an issuer) and a digital asset that can be used as hard money.

For purposes of this discussion, let's assume Bitcoin is digital money, for two reasons: first, Bitcoin was envisioned as a digital currency when it was first introduced in 2008 and, second, this approach helps us to further crystalize the concept of money. Here are the three primary functions of money (again), plus the use case for Bitcoin as money, in parallel:

1. *Store of Value:* Money can be saved and used later, because it retains its value over time—in perpetuity. Money retains its value over time because of its durable nature, meaning it doesn't rot, rust, or decay. Money also exists in finite supply (scarcity), preserving the integrity of its value.

   Bitcoin retains its value over time, because of its digital durability. Additionally, there's a finite supply of bitcoin because there will never be more than 21 million bitcoins created. Therefore, it is scarce.

2. *Unit of Account:* Money must exist in small, standardized units for less valuable exchanges and aggregated together for more valuable exchanges. The units of account must be divisible, fungible, and measurable.

   Bitcoins are standardized units that are divisible, fungible, and measurable. Each bitcoin is divisible into 100 million units, called satoshis.[23]

3. *Medium of Exchange:* Money can be used to buy and sell from one another, facilitating exchange. This is possible when money is portable (easy to transport or transmit), and when the monetary tool is widely accepted by society.

Bitcoin can be used to buy and sell from one another, facilitating exchange, peer-to-peer. This is possible because of the digital, portable nature of bitcoin. In other words, bitcoin is easy to transmit across electronic systems.

Bitcoin even cracked the code on creating digital scarcity, in the land of digital copy and paste. But beyond checking all the "money" boxes, Bitcoin offers one major, plot twist: there's no intermediary involved in its creation or circulation. Bitcoin is not issued by a bank, rather it's created by computers solving complex math problems (aka bitcoin mining).

With fiat money, trust in payments is established by government regulation of banks. With Bitcoin, trust in payments is established by blockchain, cryptography technology. Therefore, the use of Bitcoin eliminates the need for regulated banks. As a consequence, Bitcoin is geographically unconstrained; it's decentralized because of its geographically agnostic nature. Central banks have taken notice, and perhaps notes, as they explore creating their own Central Bank Digital Currency ("CBDC").

Central Bank Digital Currency

CBDC is digital currency issued directly by a nation-state's central bank, which is declared legal tender just like fiat money.[24] CBDCs are issued by the central bank, and regulated by the central bank. Currently, 60% of countries are experimenting with CBDC technology.[25] This reflects the rise of money digitalization, innovation, and a change in our future economy. Watch this space, with eyes wide open.

We only scratched the surface on digital money transformation, but there are many informative books written on the topic. A couple of suggested favorites include: *The Bitcoin Standard* by Saifedean Ammous and *Layered Money* by Nik Bhatia.

My intention for highlighting Bitcoin and CBDCs at the end of our journey through the evolution of money is to highlight the fact that things are changing. And they're changing fast! Our journey started with cowry shells and ended with cryptographic blockchain. We are traversing into the next iteration of money as our concept of money continues evolving and becoming more sophisticated over time. And as a result, our economies are evolving and becoming more sophisticated over time, too, because money enables economies to scale. We're squarely sitting in the digital economy transformation.

> *"The two greatest tests of character are wealth and poverty."*
> —*Charles A. Beard*

What Is an Economy?

An economy is a system in which goods and services are produced, sold, and bought within a country or region.[26] For purposes of this exploration, broadly speaking, there are two types of economies: the bartering economy and the money economy. It's worth mentioning, that these two types of economies are not mutually exclusive.

The Bartering Economy and the Money Economy

The bartering economy came first, and, you guessed it, is based on bartering. The bartering economy is a system where goods and services are produced and exchanged for other goods and services, without the use of money. This economic system is not the most efficient, because it's predicated on a double coincidence of wants. In other words, the two parties engaged in the exchange must both want what the other is offering - at the same time.[27] Here's an illustration of this inefficiency. Let's assume I grow potatoes, and you make shoes. We can barter, or exchange, our goods if it so happens that you want potatoes and I want shoes—at the same time. This means bartering is possible when you want to trade something you have (and don't need) for something you need (but don't have). Although the odds of someone wanting more than a few pairs of shoes are slim, unless you're Imelda Marcos (who infamously owned 3,000+ pairs of shoes).

Because of the highly inefficient nature of the bartering economy, the money economy was born. The money economy is a system in which goods and services are produced, sold, and bought with the use of money. This economic system is more efficient because it solves for the double coincidence of wants issue by using money as a medium of exchange. Here's an illustration of this efficiency. Let's assume I grow potatoes that you want, but I don't need any more shoes. So, you pay me in money for the potatoes, and I can use that money to buy the clothes I need or save that money for future purchases. *Voil*a. Problem solved. Money was the tool used to transfer value to me, in exchange for the potatoes you wanted. Everyone's happy.

Adam Smith: The Economy, Money, and Work

Who better to answer the question *What is an economy?* than the father of economics himself, Adam Smith?[28] Smith was an eighteenth-century Scottish economist, writer, and philosopher who defined economics as "an inquiry into the nature and causes of the wealth of nations."[29] Let's explore this. An economy is created in an ecosystem, which is interconnected by virtue of its financial and cultural activity. This activity includes the production, consumption, and trade of goods and services. Put differently, it's a social ecosystem of interrelated financial transactions and human practices that are influenced by a myriad of factors. Further, these financial transactions use money as a medium of exchange. As Smith put it in his renowned book, *The Wealth of Nations,* "money became the universal instrument of commerce."[30]

Because money is the universal instrument for commerce, by extension, it is also the way in which people move value around society. After all, money is an expression of value. And per the preceding, economies have a lot to do with what people value, or want. Let's assume you buy sneakers because you want them for your new workout routine. You're demanding sneakers, to the exclusion of sunglasses, for example, at a given point in time. The sneakers have a higher utility (or value) to you than the sunglasses right now. These economic decisions inform the free market. Smith refers to this concept as the *Invisible Hand*, which "is a metaphor for the unseen forces that move the free market economy. Through individual self-interest and freedom of production and consumption, the best interest of society, as a whole, are fulfilled. The constant interplay of individual pressures on market supply and demand causes the natural movement of prices and the flow of trade."[31]

In theory, capitalistic, free markets are flexible, responsive, and always seeking equilibrium. People are always voting for what they value and want, and this includes demands for innovation (in goods and services).

In order to buy goods and services, you first have to make money to pay for them. [Note: I'll avoid folding in the concept of buying on credit, for simplicity's sake.] How you decide to make money—by deciding how to spend your time and energy—also informs the market. There are three primary considerations when choosing a profession: your interests, your skills, and what the market will reward you for. How you decide to use your productivity superpowers is specific to you, which means different people will specialize and do different things (for money). Specialization is good, really good, for the economy. Here's why.

In Adam Smith's book *The Wealth of Nations*, he essentially answers the question of what causes wealth by answering: the division of labor.[32] Specialization and the division of labor are interdependent concepts. Let's unpack this. The division of labor starts with the division of a large task into smaller subtasks. From there, the smaller subtasks are assigned to different people who specialize in that specific subtask. This means that a group of individuals come together for sake of completing a large task at hand. The individual(s) specializing in the specific subtask(s) benefit from completing the task, because they are doing what interests them, what they're skilled at, and what the market will reward them for. Further, this is beneficial to the broader, larger task at hand—from an efficiency and productivity standpoint. This translates into cheaper production of the larger task (good or service), which is a win for the consumer. This is a net positive for society.

The division of labor acts as the engine for wealth creation, fueled by specialization within the labor market.[33] Individuals are happy doing what they're interested in and what they're skilled at, while the market benefits by way of increased efficiency and therefore lower priced goods and services. It follows that the more expansive a labor market is, the more expansive the division of labor can be. Smith says, "the division of labor is limited by the extent of the market."[34]

Categorically, the evolutionary timeline of economies looks similar to that of money, in that economies are also shifting focus from the tangible to the intangible. Initially, goods and services were exchanged within our neighborhoods when the coincidence of wants struck. We saw this when touching upon the barter economy earlier in this chapter. Money then enabled economies to scale and people to specialize, leading to the division of labor— resulting in increased efficiency and productivity. This unlocked the opportunity for innovation of goods and services, intangibles included. What's obvious and absolutely worth mentioning is the internet was an absolute game-changer for economic activity. The creation of the internet expanded the reach of specialized talent and therefore the division of labor because it expanded the reach of the market, plus so much more . . .

The Digital Economy

Our concept of economy changed with the introduction of the internet. The internet alchemized economies. The internet was created in 1983, which means it's technically a millennial generation invention. The World Wide Web, which made the internet available to the public, was created in 1991.[35] Also a milennial. The web democratized the internet. The internet is the infrastructure that connects computer networks together and the web organizes the information available through accessing the internet. For perspective, in 2000, 5.8% of the global population was using the internet; in 2022, 67.8% of the global population was using the internet.[36]

The internet brought financial activity online, scaling economies and profit to unprecedented proportions. The internet innovated the who, what, where, why, and how of production and consumption. Businesses are optimizing the production of their goods and services with less friction thanks to the internet. Production optimization is now easier both at the input stage (creating) and the output stage (selling). People are consuming goods and services through the internet, also known as eCommerce. Buyers and sellers now exchange goods and services over the internet, across the globe. And services now expand into electronic businesses, also known as eBusiness. Plus, businesses, both brick-and-mortar and electronic, can keep good records of all financial activity through digital accounting. Another win compliments of the internet.

The evolution of economies also saw a shift from an economy dominated by goods to an economy dominated by services and information— powered by the internet. A shift from tangible to intangible. What's more is the distinction between goods and services is now blurring. Consider how many objects (goods) you own that come bundled with services (i.e., your cell phone). This is a result of technological innovations, expanding networks, increasing utility of information, and the creation of new markets. Needless to say, economies are powerful engines for making money—the excess of which, can be spent, saved, or invested. Which leads us back to the initial question in this chapter: *What is wealth*?

From the etymological pearls of insight to socioeconomic evolution, we can appreciate the etymology of *wealth*, plus the ever-evolving relationship between wealth, money, and the economy. Money scales economies, which in turn scales wealth. The economy is an engine for wealth creation, and money acts as the fuel. Therefore, there's an obvious intertwined relationship between wealth and money, but this does not necessarily mean that lots of money simply translates into the definition of wealth. The antiquated wealth narrative deserves reimaging and redefining, on an individual level first and foremost. What's *your* wealth? After all, we saw the original, thirteenth-century definition of wealth focused on the well-being of the individual. Additionally, we saw the father of economics, Adam Smith, explain how individual interests and skills support the division of labor, which contributes to a flourishing economy (and wealth creation).

The *New Wealth Paradigm*

Naturally, the *new wealth paradigm* is predicated on how we define *wealth*. A one-dimensional definition of *wealth* leads to a narrow concept of the term, resulting in a narrow application—within our lives. A multidimensional definition of *wealth* leads to an expansive concept of the term, resulting in an expansive application—within our lives. While I'm not suggesting that every word should adopt a multidimensional and expansive definition, there are certain words that command it. And *wealth* is one of those words. We'll fully explore these different dimensions of wealth through the *5 Principles of Invisible Wealth*. But first, a look back before taking a look forward.

84 trillions of millenials

75 millin millenials

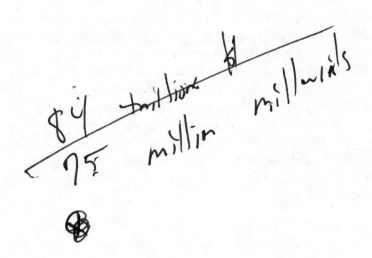

$$\frac{84,000,000,000,000}{75,000,000} =$$

So each millenial should to $1M each on TV on average

Chapter 2
A Rich Opportunity for the Unluckiest Generation

Millennials, those born between 1981 and 1996, are often referred to as the "unluckiest generation"—for reasons we'll explore in this chapter—and yet they stand to inherit over $84 trillion from their baby boomer parents in the future.[1] They are the first generation to come of age with digital technology, which is particularly noteworthy (especially after seeing how much technology impacts our concept of wealth, money, and the economy).[2] But they are also the generation who came of (professional) age during the Great Recession. This is an interesting paradox. As with everyone's life experiences, the past and present tend to influence the future. The question then becomes, how so?

Past: Why Are Millennials Called the Unluckiest Generation?

Millennials—also known as Generation Y, Digital Natives, Generation Me, Generation Rent, and Echo Boomers—are the brunt of many jokes.[3] These jokes characterize this generation as those who are self-oriented and get offended by everything, or those having a misplaced sense of arrogance and entitlement. These characteristics particularly relate to money, aka how millennials make their money, and what they spend their money on—hashtag avocado toast and almond milk latte.

Jokes aside, this generation is the largest in the United States (as of 2019), clocking in at 72.1 million people.[4] Pew Research Center projects that Generation Y will reach its peak in 2033, placing 74.9 million millennials in the United States as a result of immigration.[5] This generation is also the most researched and studied generation to date, which is fortunate for us as we reference this group for purposes of reimagining and redefining wealth. Turning to a generational cohort of people is a helpful, analytic construct for this purpose, particularly for reasons we'll explore in this chapter. We'll leverage the treasure trove of research available to understand why millennials are often referred to as the "unluckiest generation," and why they have a rich opportunity to reimagine and redefine wealth going forward.

Lucky Tailwinds

Let's start with considering what (lucky) events occurred between 1981 and 1996, besides the birthing of Gen Y. Straight out of the gate, we have a strong start with IBM releasing the personal computer in 1981. IBM's personal computer supported Microsoft as its programming language.[6] In 1984, Apple launched the Macintosh personal computer. Layering in what we learned in the previous chapter, the internet was created in 1983. The World Wide Web, which made the internet available to the public, was created in 1991.[7] Within the blink of an eye we had both the hardware and the software necessary to open up the world and to open up our minds (by virtue of access to endless information) in ways previously unimaginable. Continuing on the theme of advancements in hardware, the first commercially available handheld cell phone came to market in 1983.[8] These handheld cell phones were essentially the size of a brick. Other notable inventions of the 1980s include the Walkman, Nintendo, disposable cameras, disposable contact lenses, plus CDs and CD players.[9]

The 1980s was the decade were technology and culture started to blend together. The 1990s was the decade where this blending really advanced to a whole new level.[10]

While computers and cell phones were born in the 1980s, it wasn't until the 1990s that these inventions started to find their way into people's homes, hands, and hearts. In the early 1990s, we saw another avalanche of inventions and upgrades. For instance, in 1994, Nokia released the first mass-produced cell phone (Nokia 1011) that was smaller than the size of a brick.[11] In other words, it was more portable and therefore easier to transport. This was also the first cell phone that supported short message service (SMS) text messages.[12] When was your first text message? Mine was in 2002, eight years after the technology became widely available. I was sitting at a restaurant having breakfast with my mom before starting my freshman year of college. I moved 1,300 miles away from home to attend college, leaving my then-boyfriend behind. Distance made the heart grow fonder, so much so that he sent me a text message to say as much. I remember looking at my cell phone, perplexed as to what the text was. And even more perplexed as to how to functionally respond. Let's place a mental asterisk here and revisit the intersection between technology and relationships in Chapter 9. The point here is to illustrate that new technology and culture take time to blend, but the rate of this blending keeps accelerating as we become more and more receptive to technological advancements.

In 1998, the largest search engine in the world was born—Google. Google was created to provide a way for people to search and navigate the sea of information available across the World Wide Web.[13] Many would agree that Google played, and will continue to play, a formative role in people's personal and professional lives. Think about how much of your productivity originates from a Google search; then scale that around the world. This mighty search engine handles more than 3.5 billion searches per day.[14] Additionally, the internet brought financial activity online, scaling economies and profit to unprecedented proportions. The internet innovated the who, what, where, why, and how of production and consumption.

With so many incredible inventions coming to market in the 1980s and 1990s, why is it that millennials are considered so unlucky? They came into their teenage years with access to personal computers, cell phones, Walkmans, and disposable cameras. These items opened their world in ways their boomer parents could hardly dream of. Although, when you consider the years that millennials were finally coming into their own and into the workforce, other forces were at play—namely, economic collapse.

Unlucky Headwinds

Let's assume you were born in 1984 (speaking from experience here). This placed me as graduating high school in 2002. I started college in 2002 and graduated in 2006. Taking one year off in between undergrad and law school, I graduated law school in 2010. I, along with about 40% of other millennials,[15] went to college and ended up on the other side with a diploma and debt. Six figures of debt. Let's take a look at what was going on during the years of 2006 through 2010—as (potential) years for entering the workforce as a millennial, following the high school, college, and graduate school path.

What occurred between 2006 and 2010 was historic and referred to as the Great Recession of 2008. And there was nothing great about it. This was the largest and most severe economic decline since the Great Depression of 1929.[16] The economic landscape leading up to the recession was dynamic, and it's important to understand why. As Mark Twain said, "History never repeats itself, but it does often rhyme." Here is a brief timeline of what led to the Great Recession.

1. *Low Interest Rates, from 2001 through 2004:* The Federal Reserve lowered interest rates 11 times in 2001, in an effort to counteract a slowing economy. The slowing economy was a result of two historic events. One, the 2001 dot-com bubble burst—sending tech stocks into a sharp, downward spiral, and bringing the entire equity market with it. Two, the absolutely tragic events of 9/11 (2001). During this time, our pockets were light, and our hearts were heavy.

   In 2001, the year started with a 5.75% interest rate and the year ended with a 1.25% interest rate.[17] From there, the Fed kept interest rates low from 2001 through mid-2004.[18] Why?

   Because the Federal Reserve can influence economic activity by increasing or decreasing the interest rates, more specifically, the Fed Funds Rate (the rate banks use to lend to each other, overnight). The Fed Funds Rate then influences the Prime Rate (the rate banks use for their ideal, usually corporate, clients). Then the Prime Rate usually acts as the starting point for other interest rates—including consumer interest rates.[19] Consumer interest rates is an umbrella term that includes the rates for mortgages, small business loans, and personal loans.[20]

Typically, the lower the cost of borrowing money, the higher the odds of people borrowing money to start new businesses or buy new homes. In other words, low interest rates tend to activate financial activity. If people are starting new businesses, they are likely hiring workers, which is productive for the economy. Similarly, if people are buying new homes, they are creating earnings for all those involved in the process. Think real estate agent, loan officer, appraiser, title agent, and even the salesperson at Ikea.

Plus, new homeowners were investing their hard earned money into hard assets—real estate. Investing in real estate allows a homeowner to build equity in their property, all the while having a secure roof over their head. Homeownership is generally considered a wise investment decision because it's a pathway toward wealth creation; you can live in your home while paying down your mortgage and building equity in the asset. Then when the time comes, you can (hopefully) sell your home for a profit, which further fuels economic activity. Or you can gift or pass the home (asset) along to the next generation. This all assumes that the homeowner can afford to pay the mortgage loan that was taken out to finance the home purchase to begin with.

Based on the preceding information, we can see why people decided to invest in real estate, especially when mortgage interest rates are low. Then consider the timeframe between 2001 and 2004, when interest rates were low and so were the equity markets. Investing in bear markets is appealing to (some) investors, but we were in such a time of uncertainty (due to the dot-com bubble bursting and the tragic events of 9/11); many people were hesitant to invest in the stock market during this time. It's also worth mentioning that the government enacted policies to encourage homeownership.

This trifecta turned out to be the perfect combination for speculative buyers to come onto the scene, buying and selling ("flipping") real estate for a profit. This ended up increasing mortgage debt levels and inflating prices. Supply and demand.

2. *From Dot-com Bubble Burst to Real Estate Mega Boom:* For reasons described earlier, the real estate market boomed—largely anchored in mortgage debt. For perspective, the outstanding mortgage debt more than doubled from the beginning of 2001 to the beginning of 2008.[21]

Bear in mind that many of the people who received mortgages at low rates were able to do so because of supportive government policies, which effectively relaxed the standards for borrowing and rewarded homeownership with tax deductions and capital gains exclusions. Herein enters subprime mortgages, adjustable-rate mortgages, and mortgage-backed securities.

3. *Financial Innovations: Subprime Mortgages, Adjustable-Rate Mortgages, and Mortgage-Backed Securities:* These three financial innovations shaped the real estate mega boom. Here's a brief overview of each, and the role they played leading up to the Great Recession of 2008.

Subprime mortgages are suboptimal, relative to prime conventional mortgages. Subprime mortgages are suboptimal to the borrower because they require the payment of a higher interest rate. The silver lining, though, is that a low-credit borrower can secure financing in the form of a mortgage. Subprime mortgages are also suboptimal to the lender because they are taking on a higher risk, the risk that the low-credit borrower may default on the loan. The silver lining to the lender is that they are compensated for this risk by virtue of receiving a higher interest rate payment. The subprime mortgage expanded the reach of mortgage debt acquisition to those with lower credit scores and/or blemishes on their credit report. By 2005, subprime mortgages made up almost one-third of the mortgage debt.[22] By 2006, subprime mortgages amounted to $600 billion.[23]

Next up, let's double tap on conventional mortgages. The two primary types of conventional mortgages are: fixed rate mortgages and adjustable-rate mortgages. Fixed rate mortgages are mortgages with a fixed interest rate. This means the interest rate does not change for the life of the loan; the interest rate is static. *Adjustable-rate mortgages* are mortgages with an adjustable interest rate. This means the interest rate changes over the life of the loan; the interest rate is variable. Initially, the interest rate is set lower than that of a fixed rate mortgage, and is adjusted later based on market rates. So, a homeowner may pay a low interest rate initially, but pay a higher interest rate later, based upon the prearranged frequency and adjustment indexes.

The availability of subprime mortgages and adjustable-rate mortgages fueled the proliferation of mortgage-backed securities. Here's why.

Mortgage-backed securities ("MBS"s) are securities, backed by mortgages. A MBS is a bundle of mortgages (bought from the bank that initially granted the loans), which are packaged up into a security. The interest and principal payments that the mortgage holder pays, "passes through" to the MBS owner.[24] In effect, this freed the loan originators (the banks) from the risk of borrower default, because the banks sold the loans to the investment house and the investment house packaged the bundled mortgages (into an investment instrument). Essentially, the hot potato passed to the next person. This meant the originating bank didn't have a vested interest in the repayment of the mortgage. Human nature being what it is sometimes, this resulted in a more lax approach to lending because the risk of default passed on to someone else—the investor.

Mortgage-backed securities are derivatives, meaning they derive their value from the underlying bundle of mortgages. The strength of the mortgage-backed security is derived from the strength of the underlying mortgages. The inverse is also true.

4. *Reversing Course: The Rise of Interest Rates from 2004 through 2006:* Between 2004 and 2006, the Fed raised interest rates 17 times, increasing from 1 percent to 5.25%.[25] Why would the Fed raise rates so much when the real estate market was booming? Well, that's exactly why. As it turns out, all the lending heated the economy into inflationary territory. When the economy heats up, it is the role of the Fed to help cool things down. The Fed helps cool things down by modifying interest rates. When interest rates rise, this tightens the money supply by making it less attractive for people to borrow money for new businesses or new homes, for example.

Despite the aggressive monetary tightening from 2004 to 2006, economist Nouriel Roubini asserted that "The Fed should have tightened earlier to avoid a festering of the housing bubble early on."[26] Speaking of bubbles...

5. *Pop Goes the Weasel: The Burst of the Real Estate Bubble and Great Recession of 2008:* Come 2007, there were contending views about whether the Fed should continue increasing interest rates. By this time, increased interest rates were leading to decreased home sales and valuations, while simultaneously leading to increased inventory, plus a vicious increase in subprime mortgage and adjustable-rate mortgage defaults. As a result,

lenders started pulling back the reins on originating mortgage loans, because of these shifts in the housing market. Credit crunch. The once lax lenders weren't so lax anymore. All of these factors culminated with the bursting of the real estate bubble; thereby, initiating the Great Recession of 2008.

The writing was on the wall . . .

Now let's look at some numbers, to ground this in statistics. Losses in the housing market, and therefore in mortgage-related financial assets, had far-reaching implications. Institutional and personal balance sheets were badly hit. In 2008, the S&P 500 dropped 38.49% from the year prior.[27] In the same year, the Dow Industrial Average indices dropped 33.84%.[28] The Case-Shiller Index, which measures the change in the value of single-family homes, went from 184 in 2006, to 146 in 2009.[29] Unemployment rates went up from 4.6% in 2007, to 9.6% in 2009.[30]

In 2008, financial institutions were folding because of their overexposure to the subprime mortgage ecosystem. In the spring of 2008, JPMorgan, with the help of the Federal Reserve, acquired Bear Sterns. In the fall of 2008, Lehman Brothers filed for bankruptcy. The next day, the Federal Reserve supported AIG, sparing it from bankruptcy. Other financial institutions also sought support from the Federal Reserve.[31] AIG is an example of "too big to fail," meaning that the government bailed them out because AIG was deemed too important to the stability of the financial system and economy. This led to resentment from individuals who were left to deal with their own negative balance sheets without any help from the government. Markets were low, and tensions were high.

From Numbers to Stories

Shifting from numbers to stories, here's one for you, weaving in the millennial perspective again. Technically, the Great Recession ended in June 2009.[32] That same month, I flew from Boston to London for a summer internship at 4 Stone Chambers, in Lincoln's Inn. I was over the moon to land such an exciting opportunity, especially at the height of unemployment. 4 Stone Chambers focuses on commercial and company law, including financial services and insolvency. As luck would have it, I had a front row seat to "one of the most complex, high-stakes, and transformative situations in history" during my internship there.[33] The situation I'm referring to is the insolvency administration proceedings of Lehman Brothers International—the international, UK-based subsidiary of Lehman Brothers Holdings Inc. in the United States—that filed Chapter 11 bankruptcy in September 2008.[34]

I was assigned to the Lehman Brothers International insolvency proceedings and asked to take diligent notes. I showed up with a notebook and pen in hand, because, although laptop computers were invented during the millennial years, they just started becoming commonplace in 2008 (when laptops first outsold desktops).[35] I wrote feverishly, words and concepts I knew, but particularly—and mostly—those I didn't. This was my first exposure to the concept of a hedge fund, prime brokerage, and rehypothecation—among other new concepts. After writing as much as my hands could physically handle, I'd go back to the office to organize the scribbles. I organized concepts in a different notebook, all the while researching relevant laws and directives from the books on the bookshelf. I vividly remember a classical Spanish guitar soundtrack playing in the background. If memory serves me right, it was Narciso Yepes's *Recuerdos* album. While unscrambling words and constructing concepts, I always looked forward to 4:00 p.m. teatime, the time when everyone from the chamber came together for tea and biscuits. So charming.

My time in London, during the 4 Stone Building internship, highlighted the elegant juxtaposition between the tradition of the past, the financial innovations of the present, and the potential of the future. The past displayed by the tradition of British barristers wearing wigs to court, all the while advocating for or against innovative financial structures. The world opened up for me, literally and figuratively, and expanded my view of the future.

In August 2009, I flew back to Boston to finish my last academic year of law school. Once stateside, I started school and a new internship at Boston Consulting Group in their legal department. This internship provided (further) insight into the world of business, finance, and mergers and acquisitions. My scope of interest was expanding into the world of finance, albeit through the legal lens. In July 2010, I took the Massachusetts Bar Exam.

The Great Recession was technically over (June 2009) by the time I received the news (October 2010) that I passed the Massachusetts Bar

Exam.[36] However, the recession recovery was a slow and arduous one. This slow recovery meant employment prospects for new graduates were nil. The number of jobs lost from January 2008 onward weren't recovered until May 2014.[37] Therefore, I entered the workforce with minimal, suitable employment opportunities, which felt very anticlimactic. And the jobs that were available, were paying peanuts. Despite graduating from law school and passing the bar, I was forced to cast a wide net when applying to jobs—which included both legal and nonlegal jobs. This, my friends, is where the moniker "unluckiest generation" starts to make a whole lot of sense.

Many agree that millennials faced the worst economic odds of any other generation, which is why they are often referred to as the "unluckiest generation." Despite being the most educated and diverse generation, millennials have struggled to find their financial footing, largely due to their coming of age during the Great Recession. This meant lackluster employment opportunities, paired with staggering student loan debt, costly real estate, and difficulty securing home financing. Many millennials came into adulthood at a financial deficit—from every angle.

> *"Life is not always a matter of holding good cards, but sometimes,*
> *playing a poor hand well."*
>
> —*Jack London*

Present: Are Millennials Still Unlucky?

Today, millennials are between the ages of 27 and 42. Their childhoods were filled with Care Bears, Teenage Mutant Ninja Turtles, Rubik's Cubes, and Game Boys.[38] Their teenage years were filled with disposable cameras, the joy of call waiting, AOL chat rooms, plus buying CDs and magazines. Their 20s included Myspace, Facebook, flip phones, and Apple iPods. Millennials grew lock step with the digital transformation. Lucky. But they also experienced the Great Recession during (professionally) formative years. Not lucky. So where does this place this generation today?

Over time, the reputation of millennials shifted from self-oriented and entitled, to optimistic and resilient. This diverse and well-educated cohort faced unchartered territory and economic headwinds, which required them to navigate a dynamic landscape. And generally speaking, they've navigated this landscape with hopefulness and creative adaptability. Additionally, it turns out that their preference for avocado toast and almond milk lattes didn't come from a place of entitlement, but from consideration—for one's health and the health of the environment. As Albert Einstein said, "When you change the way you look at things, the things you look at change."

Millennials faced structural changes, both personally and professionally, as a result of technological innovations and the Great Recession. Some optimal, some suboptimal. These changes required agile responses to external forces, while perhaps delaying or reorganizing the hallmarks of adulthood. For example, the delay of getting married, purchasing a home, and having children. More than half of millennials are not married, and the ones who got married, got married later in life (relative to prior generations).[39] Fewer than half of millennials are homeowners.[40] A little more than half of millennial women have given birth, and did so later on in life (relative to prior generations).[41] These adulthood delays are largely a consequence of financial woes. Bloomberg Wealth even went on to say, "Millennials are running out of time to build wealth."[42] The clock is ticking, and time waits for no one.

The Deloitte Global 2022 Gen Z and Millennial Survey provides us with the top financial concerns and statistics for these generations. With a continued focus on our millennials friends: 47% live paycheck-to-paycheck; 31% aren't confident they'll be able to retire with financial comfort; 33% have taken on an additional job (either part-time or full-time), and 29% simply don't feel financially secure.[43]

Most recently, millennials experienced their second recession, within the first half of their lives, due to the pandemic. Fortunately, or unfortunately, this wasn't their first rodeo. The good news is millennials doubled their wealth since the start of the pandemic, from $4.55 trillion to $9.13 trillion.[44] This is a staggering statistic. But when you take a peek behind the curtain, you'll see this statistic is somewhat theatrical. First, the ability to double wealth in such a short amount of time lends itself to the fact that there was not much wealth to begin with. For example, it's easier to double $10 to $20 than to double $100 to $200. Despite the doubling, baby boomer parents are still worth eight times as much as millennials. This older generation saw their wealth expand to $71 trillion since the pandemic began.[45]

Second, while wages are now higher for millennials, compared to previous generations, so is the cost of living. The cost of living looks even worse when you consider current inflationary pressures. That said, the net amount of income available for saving and investing is much lower, which is why millennial wealth remains hard hit. Third, the recent doubling of millennial wealth is largely a result of the increasing value of real estate. This makes sense when you consider the fact that 35.6% of millennials' net worth is tied up in real estate.[46]

The landscape remains dynamic.

> *"Reject your sense of injury and the injury itself disappears."*
>
> —*Marcus Aurelius*

Future: A Rich Opportunity for the Unluckiest Generation

Millennials have, and will continue to, shape the economy based on their unique circumstances and characteristics—as compared to times past. As they embark into their prime spending years, they'll inform the market as to what is valuable, or not; influencing the supply/demand dynamics of the economy. Millennials are reevaluating and reprioritizing value (quantitative) predicated on values (qualitative)—as most of us are. This is incredibly important when considering the upcoming Great Wealth Transfer. More on this in Chapter 3.

The Great Wealth Transfer refers to the transferring of $84 trillion of wealth, from the baby boomer generation to millennials (and younger generations, the grandkids). This will make millennials the richest generation in the United States.[47] The wealth accumulated by generations past will be brought forward into the hands of millennials at present, to influence the economy of the future. There's a changing of the guards underway. Needless to say, there's extraordinary potential for millennials to influence the economy and the trajectory of the future.

For example, millennials are already shaping the (sharing) economy by placing dollars behind ride shares over car ownership. Of course, you don't need to inherit large sums of money to influence the financial and cultural activity of the economy. As the old adage goes, there is power in numbers. Many millennials are bringing their agile, adaptive, optimistic, resilient, creative, and well-educated perspectives to the table, with digital wallet in hand. That said, they're placing a premium on intangible assets, and spending with values in mind. As a result, corporations are pivoting, plus new businesses are coming online to accommodate these demands.[48] The millennial generation is leading the way in reimaging and redefining wealth, through reimagining the value of values.

At this point, the genie is out of the bottle.

"Luck is what happens when preparation meets opportunity."

—*Seneca*

Chapter 3
We Can't Put the Genie Back in the Bottle

illennials aren't the only ones rethinking what they value, and therefore rethinking how they define wealth-but the world collectively, too. This theme is omnipresent. We are in the midst of a huge paradigm shift, and this shift caught exponential wind as we turned inward and reflected—during the forced pressures and pauses of the pandemic. This, we know. Now, let's delve into the *greatness* that resulted from these pressures and pauses, namely: the Great Wealth Transfer, the Great Migration, and the Great Resignation, all of which are fueling the Great Restructuring.

As a preview, this includes technological advancements, entrepreneurial spirit animals, innovation, and invention. We're currently living in a dynamic time that commands dynamic change. And as it turns out, we can't put the genie back in the bottle.

The Great Wealth Transfer

Over the coming decades, the Great Wealth Transfer will place $84 trillion into the hands of millennials (and younger generations) from the hands of baby boomers. This will be the greatest wealth transfer in history.[1]

As previously mentioned, the recipients of this wealth are spending and investing through the filter of their values. Businesses are pivoting in response to this wealth transfer, rethinking business models and branding. It's necessary to be relevant and attractive to the new wealth holders in order to capture market share for these mighty dollars. There's clear recognition and acknowledgement that millennials are generally interested in values-based spending and values-based investing.² Businesses are interested in how millennials will spend their newfound money, while wealth managers and advisors (the world I come from) are interested in how millennials will invest their newfound money. The values of millennials are coloring the future economy. Furthermore, money is the instrument that fuels the economy. Adam Smith taught us this. And an economy is, after all, an ecosystem interconnected by financial and cultural activity. The financial and cultural tides are a turning.

Millennials, businesses, and wealth managers aren't the only one's planning for the Great Wealth Transfer, but of course, the boomers themselves. While no one likes to talk about it, it is important to discuss the investment strategy and structuring of assets ahead of one's demise. This is a delicate topic and discussion, but one that is beneficial to all involved. These conversations open the door to multigenerational family discussions regarding money and wealth, which is profoundly valuable. Conversations about unexpected turn of events became commonplace during the pandemic, because mortality was at the forefront of everyone's mind.

The Great Migration

Let's start this section with a Great Migration anecdote.

On January 25, 2020, I flew from Switzerland back to New York City. After a week in Switzerland meeting and connecting with inspiring people, I flew back to the United States, without any awareness of the impending pandemic. A month later, I was pegged to travel to Finland and Estonia. By February, there were headlines and hesitations relating to the novel virus. I contemplated my trip back to Europe, because of the growing fear around travel. Ultimately, I decided to hop on a plane, as planned. On March 3, 2020, I flew from Finland back to New York City after a conference called Kinnernet. A new Kinnernet friend, originally coming from Israel, gave me a face mask to wear on my flight back home. This day, this flight, was the first time I wore a mask, and it wasn't the last. I was one of four people on the plane wearing a mask, and I felt a bit silly about it. After touching down in New York City, things changed, and they changed rapidly. On March 12, 2020, nine days after coming home, New York issued a state of emergency executive order. The next day, Friday the 13th, marked my last day in my Manhattan office. On March 21, 2020, I went to New Hampshire—indefinitely—with a carry-on suitcase in hand. I rode the train from Penn Station (New York City) to South Station (Boston), all the while wearing two masks, a hat, glasses, and socks pulled up over my pants. The (unrational) rationale was to have the least amount of skin exposed as possible, because at this point we didn't know exactly how this virus was transmitted and contracted. We all remember the days, circumstances, and feelings of the first quarter, in 2020 (and all that followed).

What does this anecdote have to do with the Great Migration? Everything. The beginning of 2020 catapulted us into new territory, literally and figuratively. America migrated to rural and suburban areas, to different cities, and, most notably, online.

Migrating

During the first month of the pandemic, net moves out of Manhattan tripled. Additionally, net moves out of Brooklyn, Chicago, and Los Angeles doubled. During the first year of the pandemic, specifically March 2020 through February 2021, moves from dense urban areas to rural and suburban areas jumped 17%.[3] Change of address forms let us know that permanent moves, in March 2020, jumped 15% nationwide.[4] Astonishing. Permanent decisions were made during hazy moments. The novel virus was moving quickly, initiating permanent and semipermanent moves everywhere. Naturally, people sought seclusion and space, along with peace of mind. Rural and suburban areas, by definition, provide less density and more space—offering a more comfortable quarantining experience.

So, where did everyone go? Mostly to the rural and suburban areas near the dense urban areas where they lived . . . and worked. Both households and businesses, homes and offices, moved from dense city centers to lower density suburban zip codes. This phenomenon is called the "donut effect."[5] Quite clever. The donut effect, in this context, refers to the rising prices of properties in the suburbs relative to the prices of properties in city centers.

People also ventured to different states. Florida saw a 34% increase in new-comers, and North Carolina, South Carolina, Arizona, and Texas received similar levels of inbound.[6] At the time, a lot of my private wealth management clients relocated to their second homes in the Hamptons, Upstate New York, Florida, New Mexico, and Wyoming. Ultimately, some clients turned their secondary homes into primary homes, and their primary homes into second-ary homes. This was advantageous for my New York City clients, because they moved from a high tax residency to a lower tax residency. Others were purchasing new, secondary homes. For those interested in buying, low inter-est rates were supportive. Those with the means had the option to pivot and purchase. Those who didn't found novel ways to find seclusion, space, and solace from the novel virus.

As a quick but relevant aside, the Great "Wealth" Migration is currently underway across the world, as millionaires are on the move. In 2022, it's projected that 88,000 millionaires will move to a new country. The coun-tries attracting the most millionaires: United Arab Emirates, Australia, and Singapore.[7]

Pivoting back to the United States, those considered financially wealthy were mostly flocking to Florida. The Sunshine State offered—you guessed it, sunshine—and no income tax, making it an attractive option. In 2020, Florida saw a 20,263 net inflow of high earners (those making $200,000 or more per year).[8] In 2020, New York saw a nearly 20,000 net outflow of high earners, the highest of all 50 states. I'm included in this statistic, because I moved from New York City to Miami in 2020. More on this later.

In March 2020, interest rates were 1.10%. In March 2021, one year later, interest rates were 0.07%.[9] That said, mortgage rates were really attractive. When mortgage rates are attractive, so is buying real estate with credit. This we now know. As the Fed eased monetary policy, the housing market tightened.

The housing market tightened for a few reasons. First, moving during a pandemic isn't ideal. Logistically speaking, house shopping during a pan-demic isn't optimal, and neither is hiring movers, or anything else that goes along with relocating. For this reason, many people opted to sit tight in their homes, and wait out the storm. Second, as a natural consequence, this meant the number of homes on the market was low. Plus, new construction builds were put on hold. And what happens when there's low supply, yet high demand? Price inflation. Third, buyers were eager to improve their living conditions by purchasing homes with more space; inside, outside, or both. Resonance with our residence improves our well-being. That said, given the sensitivities surrounding the pandemic and the search for solace, many turned a blind eye to price inflation, especially because interest rates were so low (as a counterbalance to the higher-than-normal real estate prices).

And which generation was the driving force behind this boost in the real estate demand during the pandemic? You guessed it—millennials. In 2019, millennials accounted for 38% of home buyers.[10] In 2020, millennials accounted for 37% of home buyers.[11] And in 2021, millennials accounted for 43% of home buyers.[12] [One caveat regarding these statistics: this information came from the National Association of Realtors, and they classify millennials as those born from 1980–1998; we initially defined millennials as those born between 1981 and 1996.]

Millennials were, and remain, the driving force behind real estate purchases. While the pandemic acted as a catalyst into homeownership, this catalyst aligned with the fact that this generation was already coming into the homeownership stage of life. So, the timing was right based upon stage of life—for the largest generation to date. People might be scratching their heads, thinking, how can a financially insecure generation afford to purchase real estate? Great question. In some cases, millennials recieved financial gifts from relatives willing to pay the down payment on their new homes.[13] This shows us that baby boomer parents are starting to loosen their purse strings to help their adult children, financially. This is a preview into the power behind the Great Wealth Transfer; as the boomer generation starts transferring wealth to the next generation via *inter vivos* gifts. *Inter vivos* is a Latin term meaning a gift between the living.

Migrating Online

During the pandemic, people migrated to rural and suburban areas, to different cities, and most notably—online, which is why I believe the Great

Migration also includes the (fuller) migration online. In fact, the migration online was a prerequisite for those moving geographies—technology enabled remote work. As my clients migrated to their second or new homes, so did our meetings; our meetings migrated from my Manhattan office to Zoom. This migration, or transition, happened overnight. My last day in the office was on a Friday, and it was business as usual on Monday—except, it was not so usual. Companies pivoted online at lightening speed, and so did their employees, clients, and customers. It's really remarkable. Of course, initial glitches and awkward moments peppered our Zoom experiences. "You're on mute" became a meme, with cultural force. Memes aside, productivity was also a force; employees didn't miss a beat. Businesses and individuals came to the quick realization that the move to remote work enabled the move to remote geographies. And vice versa.

The Great Resignation

Forty-seven million people. This was the population size of Spain in 2021.[14] Forty-seven million people. This was also the population size that quit their jobs (in the United States) in 2021.[15] This pandemic-era labor trend is referred to as the "Great Resignation."

The year 2021 was interesting, because we were still in the throes of the pandemic, yet the economy was picking up steam. In the second quarter of 2021, gross domestic product (GDP) returned to pre-pandemic levels.[16] Gross domestic product picked up as a result of increased demands for goods and services, driven by consumer spending. Consumer spending typically accounts for 70% of GDP. Pent up demand plus government stimulus payments placed more money into the hands of consumers, and thereafter, into the economy. People were ready for haircuts and dining out, among many other things. Naturally, haircuts require hairdressers and dining out requires cooks and wait staff. In other words, the need for workers increased and the need increased across sectors. While more jobs were coming online (literally and figuratively), more people were quitting their jobs. Curious.

Home residency wasn't the only thing people were reconsidering during the pandemic; they were reconsidering their jobs as well. Reevaluating, reconsidering, retiring, and resigning were the employment themes over the past few years. Why? The title of a Pew Research Article sums it up perfectly: "Majority of workers who quit their jobs in 2021 cite low pay, no opportunities for advancement, feeling disrespected."[17] These reasons are pretty self-explanatory, and likely reasons we can all relate to—at some point or another in our careers. While the first reason is very easy to quantify, the last two are not. Let's start with the quantifiable reason first, and work our way through the less quantifiable reasons thereafter. Spoiler alert: millennials (and Gen Z's) led this movement, too.

First, millions of people quit their jobs in 2021, because of low pay.[18] 37% said low pay was a major reason for their departure, and 26% said it was a minor reason for their departure, totaling to 63%. Bear in mind, millennials (in large part) entered the workforce on the heels of the Great Recession, which meant most started their careers earning lower-than-normal pay. This had a meaningful impact on the amount of compensation earned thereafter, when you consider the fact that salaries often increase by about 3% per year. For perspective, the average millennial lost around 13% of their earnings between the years of 2005 and 2017.[19] Reduced earnings were largely a result of the slow and arduous recovery from the Great Recession. As the saying goes, timing is everything. Which is exactly why when 2021 rolled around, this generation jumped at the golden opportunity to level up their pay.

Job seekers finally felt confident about the job market, for two primary reasons: wages were high and unemployment numbers were low. In 2021, wage growth reached 4.5%, which is the highest it's been since 2001.[20] Additionally, in 2021, the unemployment rate dropped as low as 3.9%.[21] For perspective, the unemployment rate peaked the year prior, at 14.7% in 2020.[22]

Initially, it was the younger employees who were most eager to throw in the towel with their employers. Gen Z's (those born between 1997 and 2012) are the workforce newbies. This young generation barely had a moment to finish their coffees at their desks, let alone find their way up the corporate ladder before an exciting job market presented itself in 2021. At this point, this Gen Z had the least amount of time, energy, and loyalty established with their employers. Despite lots of movement among these workforce newbies, it was the millennials who made waves within the labor markets. Millennials were incredibly attractive hires to employers because these digital natives had valuable work experience under their belt. By the end of 2021, wage growth went up 13.1% and 9.2% from the year prior, for Gen Z's and millennials, respectively.[23]

Second, millions of people quit their jobs in 2021, because of the lack of opportunities to advance their careers. Among those who did, 33% said low opportunity for advancement was a major reason for their departure, and 30% said it was a minor reason, totaling to 63%.[24] This reason makes sense when you consider that most people who quit their jobs in 2021 were Gen Z's or millennials. In other words, in the formative phase of their careers and wanting to see a fruitful road ahead. Staying put became much less compelling without visibility into future career opportunities—especially when there were so many new opportunities available elsewhere. Additionally, many of these new opportunities were location agnostic because many jobs turned remote during the pandemic. The Great Migration online opened up a world of professional opportunity and growth—literally.

Third, millions of people quit their jobs in 2021, because they felt disrespected. Among those who did, 35% said feeling disrespected was a major reason for their departure, and 21% said it was a minor reason, totaling to 56%.[25] Feeling disrespected looks different for everyone, given the highly subjective nature of this emotion. During this historical time, divisive stances were taken on everything from health to politics—highly charged topics. We were all experiencing emotional upheaval in our lives during the pandemic; the extent of which varied person to person. That said, this is not a one-size-fits-all discussion. Nonetheless, it's an incredibly important reason to consider because it played such a big role in the Great Recession, per Pew's research.

There's clearly a holistic tilling of the soil going on.

> *"The pandemic brought the future of work into the present of work."*
> —*Anthony Klotz,*
> *who coined the term*
> *the "Great Resignation"*[26]

The Great Restructuring

It's only natural that the incoming Great Wealth Transfer, paired with the Great Migration and Great Resignation, would lead to the inevitable— Great Restructuring. The Great Restructuring has individuals and businesses playing four-dimensional chess, mostly with themselves—as they seek to future-proof and optimize their positioning in the world. Considerations include the current, unfamiliar landscape with a lens toward the inevitable transformations of the future. What we learned over the past couple of years is that the rules of the game can change on the drop of a dime, and the ability to pivot is now a—necessary—superpower.

> *"We learn geology the morning after the earthquake."*
> —*Ralph Waldo Emerson*

Individuals and businesses are reinventing and restructuring themselves. As we saw earlier, an economy is a social ecosystem that transforms based on changes in financial activity and cultural activity. What individuals and businesses decide to consume and produce influences the shape and texture of the economy. This is why the rethinking, reinventing, and, ultimately, restructuring of individuals and businesses is impacting the economy accordingly—Digital Darwinism is in full force.

Restructuring looks different for different entities, because of the uneven impact the pandemic had across people, geographies, and industries. For individuals, many are reskilling for new jobs, starting new businesses, and/or cultivating their own personal brands. For businesses, many are reskilling their workforce, revisiting their business models, and/or reimagining their company brand. The restructuring path requires the reevaluation of purpose, principles, and values. One thing's for sure, human capital is absolutely necessary for implementing and sustaining these structural changes. With a tight workforce, finding talent might seem like a job in and of itself. For businesses, the right talent adds to the bottom line, while also adding to the richness of company culture—which is becoming more and more of a competitive advantage these days (both for attracting loyal customers and rockstar employees).

Human capital is arguably the most valuable asset a business has as they restructure. This intangible asset ultimately reveals itself by way of profitability. Although, human capital is becoming harder to find for a multitude of reasons. One reason businesses are finding it harder to find talent is because the entrepreneurial spirit animals are alive and well.

Spiritus Animalis is Latin for "the breath that awakens the human mind."

Entrepreneurial Spirit Animals

Lions and tigers and bears, oh my. These days, the *entrepreneurial spirit animals* are alive and well, and roaming the economic ecosystem in full force. Let's define both *entrepreneur* and *animal spirits*, in order to fully appreciate the phrase *entrepreneurial spirit animals*.

Entrepreneurs are people who start companies that provide a good or service, which typically isn't already available in the marketplace (as compared to small business owners whose business is typically already available in the marketplace). That said, entrepreneurs are considered bigger risk takers because they navigate unchartered territory. Also, entrepreneurs typically have an eye toward short-term success (thereafter, perhaps funding the next entrepreneurial endeavor), whereas small business owners typically have an eye toward long-term, stable profitability.

Animal spirits is a term coined by John Maynard Keynes, a famous British economist, in his 1936 book *The General Theory of Employment, Interest and Money*.[27] In this book, Keynes refers to animal spirits as the (invisible) forces at play within an economy, specifically, the psychological and emotional factors that drive economic decision-making by people within an economy. Animal spirits represent the emotional temperament toward the economy at a given point in time. Thus, when people feel confident and hopeful about the state of the economy, they are more inclined to spend and invest. This, in turn, propels the health of the economy even further; like a self-fulfilling prophecy of sorts (of course, only to an extent and with limitations). The perception and belief in the health of the economy, fosters more health of the economy.

Consider this example. Let's say that you're really thriving at work right now, and up for a big promotion, which means a big bonus. This big promotion and bonus are a result of you and your company's exceptional success over the past five years. You and your company are reaping huge profits because the economy is healthy and there's lots of confidence in the strength of the markets. And it gets even better, because your investment portfolio performance is excellent; you're seeing double-digit returns in the green. Given these factors, you feel very comfortable booking that trip to Lisbon or Paris, which you always dreamed of. This would be an example of positive animal spirits being alive and well. Animal spirits are conceptually similar to spirit animals.

Therefore, *entrepreneurial spirit animals* are the psychological and emotional factors driving entrepreneurs to do what they do: their archetypal essence. An entrepreneurial founder may identify with the archetypal traits of a lion. These traits include wanting to be the king of the jungle, leading the way for others by exuding power, confidence, and courage. Lions lead with heart and are respected by those around them.

Spirit animal idioms are sprinkled throughout our vocabulary. Take the familiar saying to "work like a horse." This is an example of an archetypal spirit animal. Horses are known as hard workers, with lots of energy and perseverance. Another familiar saying is to "work like a dog." Dogs are known to work tirelessly until they achieve their goals.

So, how alive and well are these entrepreneurial spirit animals? The answer is, very, and for a handful of reasons. Let's consider why anyone would want to take on the risk of starting their own company. First, is the obvious: you're your own boss. And when you're your own boss, you call the shots, which includes mapping the opportunities ahead and being in charge of your own growth trajectory. Second, you have the ability to control your financial security, without capped upside potential. Third, you have the flexibility to design your own work-life balance, well suited to your personality and circumstances. Fourth, you can create a company based on your own purpose, principles, and values. Fifth and final, you may achieve higher meaning, purpose, and satisfaction from your work, because it's entirely tailored to your own interests and motivations.

Notice the first three reasons for entrepreneurship completely solve for the top three reasons why a "majority of workers quit their jobs in 2021 cite low pay, no opportunities for advancement, feeling disrespected," per Pew's article, previously discussed.

With these reasons fresh in mind, it's easy to see why millennials are so inclined to pursue entrepreneurship. Entering the workforce on the heels of the Great Recession, millennials were thrown off traditional paths. Therefore, right out of the gate, they were navigating unchartered territory, roaming the wild without a map. Their familiarity with the unknown, and their courage to approach it, is embedded in their archetypal essence. Also, they are motivated to make money because they started their careers at a financial deficit (larger student loan debt and lower than average wages). Plus, as digital natives, their comfort level with technology makes them well-suited to place their paws to computer keyboard, wherever in the world that may be.

Entrepreneurs often create companies motivated by social values and driven by spirit animals. Speaking of animals, let's look at Bumble as an example. In 2014, Whitney Wolfe Herd founded Bumble, a female-focused dating app dedicated to women making the first move. Why did the queen bee of Bumble create this first-of-its-kind dating app? Because she wanted to flip the script on dating dynamics and empower women to make the first move.[28] The app was created by women, for women. Bumble's novel approach to dating apps made Whitney Wolfe Herd the youngest self-made billionaire in the world.

This is one example of an entrepreneur creating a good or service that influenced the shape and texture of society. Judgments aside—whether you're in favor of dating apps or not—there's no denying that they are influencing society in a significant way.

Bumble's success potential was possible because of the internet, smartphones, and smartphone apps. That said, we're seeing new marketplaces coming online, standing on the shoulders of prior inventions and innovations. Another example of new marketplaces coming online are all the businesses using platforms such as YouTube, Instagram, Twitter, and LinkedIn. These online platforms create new ecosystems for wealth generation.

> *"Don't think money does everything or you are going*
> *to end up doing everything for money."*
>
> —*Voltaire*

Digital Darwinism

Speaking of animals, let's pivot to the concept of *Digital Darwinism*, which is the application of Darwin's Theory of Evolution to the digital economy. This term was coined by American author, Evan I. Schwartz, in 1999 when he recognized that technology and society were evolving faster than companies could naturally adapt.[29] Companies that don't quickly adapt, fail. This is natural selection, just like we see in the animal kingdom. Established companies have established technological infrastructure already in place, making it difficult and clunky to adopt new technologies and ways of doing business. Businesses with legacy infrastructure may be more resistant to adopting digital service delivery, updating payment systems (e.g., two-factor authentication) or enhancing cybersecurity protocol. These structural considerations pose big hurdles for established businesses to adapt, especially when compared to start-ups—but fairness has never been a consideration for survival of the fittest. Corporate complacency meets earnest entrepreneurs, and there's nowhere to hide.

Consumers are now demanding new technologies, thereby further fueling digital transformation. People are buying from, and doing business with, companies that are digitally relevant. For example, consumers (and employees, for that matter) expect companies to provide up-to-date user experiences, with optimized security and safety measures in place. As a consequence, it's imperative that businesses transform lockstep with this digital transformation. "Adapt or die." Draconian, yet accurate.

In some cases, adapting requires restructuring through new business models. Restructuring, in its most aggressive form, comes in the form of a merger or acquisition ("M&A"). In 2021, the merger and acquisition industry had a record year, with over $5 trillion of global activity.[30] Many companies (across all sectors) are turning to M&A to implement and accelerate digital transformation, with the goal of increasing growth and profitability.[31] Digital Darwinism spares no one; it touches all sectors and all types of companies, both private and public, small and large.

After considering all these *great* circumstances, at this point, it's fair to say that we can't put the genie back in the bottle.

Value most –

Want more of –
- ORDER
- time outside

Part II

We can't put the genie back in the bottle, but why would we want to? After all, the genie grants wishes, which begs the question: What are your wishes? In other words, what do you value most and want more of? After all, we are wealthy when we have an abundance of what we value. This book is an invitation to reimagine and redefine what wealth means to *you,* within the context of our present-day world, because, as it turns out, wealth is much more multifaceted than the antiquated narrative might have you think. It's time to expand the concept and definition of wealth, into the world of *Invisible Wealth.*

> *"A person's worth is measured by the worth of what he values."*
> —*Marcus Aurelius*

Part II of this book introduces and explores the *5 Principles of Invisible Wealth*: wealth of money and investment; wealth of health and quality of life; wealth of knowledge, status, and influence; wealth of time, energy, and experience; and wealth of relationships with self and others. Each principle is fundamentally familiar yet deserves revisiting as we enter into the *new wealth paradigm.* These principles highlight the ways in which we are

49

becoming increasingly comfortable with pegging value to intangible assets, digital assets included. The universe of value is evolving, as new innovations develop. With the evolution in our concept of value comes the evolution in our concept of wealth.

Chapter 4
The 5 Principles of Invisible Wealth

Like a bird migrating south for winter, in November 2020, I flew from New York City to Miami with two suitcases in hand and with the intention of staying for three months. Three months turned into six months, six months turned into nine months, and nine months turned into twelve months, and counting. Never in my wildest dreams would I imagine living in Miami all the while working my New York City job. I also never imagined many of my friends would also make the same migration, placing familiar faces in unfamiliar places. It took me nearly a year to decide whether I migrated or, in fact, moved. One compelling consideration in my decision to stay—and officially move to Miami—was Mayor Francis Suarez's motto "How can I help?", which reverberates throughout the sunny city.

During this transition from migration to move, from temporary to permanent, I was forced to get crystal clear on what I value. To begin with, I was living with less because all my belongings (save for two suitcases) were in storage back in New York City. I was maxing out minimalism and finding it quite liberating. As it turns out, having fewer things didn't negatively impact my life—in fact, it improved it. This is just one obvious example of me rethinking and getting clear on what I value. What was more meaningful was the rethinking and reimagining of my finances, health, quality of life, knowledge, status, influence, time, energy, experiences, and relationships. It led me to ask what was truly important for experiencing life to the fullest? What resources are most valuable, and how to best attain, maintain, and grow these resources? Circumstances required me to ask these questions while looking at myself in the proverbial mirror.

And the funny thing is, this wasn't my first rodeo. I moved 10 times by the age of 20, and yet never thought so deeply about my values, and by extension, my concept of wealth. But this migration turned move, coupled with the current paradigm shift, had me facing facts head on—as many of us are.

I lived out my own Great Migration, and in the process, underwent a metaphysical transformation—one that redefined my values. This transformation, when layered on top of my experiences as an immigrant, my nomadic upbringing, life as a millennial woman, and the insights collected over the years as a wealth adviser, all led me to new ideas on how to reconceptualize wealth. Through this process, the concept of *Invisible Wealth* took shape, and along with it, the five principles that embody this concept.

> *"A person's worth is measured by the worth of what he values."*
> —*Marcus Aurelius*

While recharacterizing and reprioritizing what I value, I started to notice that this transformation was taking place for others, too. This reprioritization didn't start with the pandemic, but it certainly was accelerated by it.

We, individually and collectively, are living in interesting times, experiencing a paradigm shift in wealth, money, and in the economy. We're unlocking utility and monetizing in new ways within the arena of intangible assets, although this is not unprecedented. A well-recognized example of intangible assets is the concept of *intellectual property*. Many are familiar with the value of intangible creations, born from the mind, which are claimed and protected through copyrights, patents, and trademarks. The notion of intangible value is scaling into new arenas, because of our increasing comfort level with; the invisible makers and markers of wealth.

Despite the inability to touch intangibles, such as ideas, we do see the consequential manifestation of these invisible forces, and they're powerful! When we actualize our ideas, we receive a return on that investment.

A return on investment can come in the form of increased value, whether that be money or lessons learned.

To ground this point in business terms, consider this example: an entrepreneur thinks of an idea and wants to actualize the idea into a lucrative business. The entrepreneur researches, home in on product–market fit, creates a prototype, and develops a go-to-market strategy. This venture could be lucrative, or it could be a flop; regardless, it will yield lessons learned. Either way, there is value creation. While at Fidelity, I developed a proof of concept and a prototype for an enterprise solution. After pitching this idea to the leadership team, it was advanced into early incubation. From there, I partnered with a sharp-witted team to further develop the concept, product–market fit, and prototype. Ultimately, the concept didn't progress into advanced incubation, but I gained valuable insights and lessons that will contribute to future endeavors.

As a society, we acknowledge and celebrate the tangible and visible markers of wealth. Think: big homes, new cars, and designer shoes. Although, in portfolio construction terms, many are reallocating from an overweight in tangible wealth to an overweight in intangible wealth. The concept of *Invisible Wealth* provides the opportune framework to help us explore what it means to be *wealthy*.

In my estimation, true wealth is invisible.

> *"The real measure of our wealth is how much we'd be worth if we lost all our money."*
>
> —*John Henry Jowett*

In the chapters that follow, we'll delve into the *5 Principles of Invisible Wealth*, which are:

P1: Wealth of Money and Investment
P2: Wealth of Health and Quality of Life
P3: Wealth of Knowledge, Status, and Influence
P4: Wealth of Time, Energy, and Experiences
P5: Wealth of Relationships, with Self and Others

These five principles are well-known concepts, but they absolutely require revisiting and redefining, because of the technological innovations and societal shifts underway (impacting how we make, spend, and invest money).

Money is a resource; health is a resource; knowledge is a resource; status is a resource; influence is a resource; time is a resource; energy is a resource; experiences are resources, and relationships are resources. That said, wealth can be defined as an abundance of resources, including but not limited to, the resource of money. All these resources have the potential to compound over time. The compounding of invested money is a, concept we are familiar with, yet we don't talk often enough about the compounding potential (and therefore increased quantity and quality) of these other resources.

Plus, the biggest financial decisions you'll ever make, likely won't relate directly to money and investment, but instead to what you eat, what information you consume, who you spend your time with, and if/who you marry. Here's a peek behind the curtain, as a preview of the *5 Principles of Invisible Wealth*, which we will explore more fully in the following chapters.

The Wealth of Money and Investment

Principle 1 (P1) addresses the reality that money is a necessity that affords us security, freedom, and choice. The more money we have, the more safety, flexibility, and optionality we have. Although the book focuses on the qualitative nature of wealth, I do acknowledge and encourage the attainment of financial wealth. As a certified wealth advisor, I thoroughly understand how the accumulation of financial wealth provides safety, independence, and opens doors to rich potential. Plus, money enhances the most important things in life.

In this chapter, we'll discuss the wealth journey and how the wealth of money and investment are interconnected. The best way to grow your money is by keeping it "invisible" or, in other words, invested; to have and to hold is greater than to show and to tell. When money remains invisible, or invested, it has the potential to grow and compound. Compounding interest is the money you earn from your investment's interest. Sounds appealing, right? And it is; so much so that many credit Albert Einstein with calling it *the eighth wonder of the world*.

Thereafter, we'll double tap into a broader interpretation of the compounding interest concept by highlighting that not only does the account holder benefit from exponential financial growth, but also perhaps others do, too—truly drawing on compounding interests, by many (versus one).

2   The Wealth of Health and Quality of Life

Principle 2 (P2) embraces the fact that health is foundational to both creating and enjoying wealth. The pandemic's forced pressures and pauses put health front and center for us all. With health top of mind, we dove into the treasure trove of research and insight available, relating to the optimization of health. In our search for optimal health, experts and intuition let us know that physical health is important, but so is mental and spiritual health. While there are visible indications of health (e.g., weight), what's often more telling are the invisible indications of health (e.g., microbiome, blood sugar, and stress levels). Advancements in healthcare technology are providing visibility into the invisible markers of health, through wearable technology such as smart watches, fitness trackers, and clothing with built-in tech for health monitoring. There's now a wealth of big data available to predict and prevent ailments. Therefore, we'll highlight and discuss the ways we are reimagining our health practices, and how these practices are tightly correlated to quality of life.

Thereafter, we'll expand the conversation from quantitative health insights to qualitative daily practices, which ultimately create the story of your life. This requires placing thoughtful attention on the way life has completely changed due to technological advancements and societal shifts. Much of our life has replatformed online, where business and social now take place virtually, too. Business is not only possible but also productive via Zoom. And social media enables countless more social interactions. Given that much of our lives are now online, this changes how we live in the day-to-day, providing much more autonomy over how we manage our time. On the opposite side of the coin, addiction to technology is a real threat, which is why considering a media diet should be part of everyone's daily practice.

This shift online has huge implications, including the fact that it allows us to become location agnostic. Being location agnostic means that talent and relationships have the potential to live anywhere (beyond just the mega-metropolis areas). Therefore, people now consider living in locations that previously were not on their radars, and optimizing quality of life as a result. Further, as we reorganize ourselves across the globe, it's worth mentioning the interest in our collective health, in addition to our individual health. Since March 2020, we are much more concerned with how others are tending to their health, realizing that the health of others can influence and impact the health of self—this includes physical, mental, and spiritual health.

The Wealth of Knowledge, Status, and Influence

Principle 3 (P3) dives into knowledge, and specifically the use of knowledge, which has a powerful relationship with wealth, status, and influence. This we intuitively know, but it deserves further discovery. Knowledge is a tool to accumulate wealth; wealth and status are interlinked, because you can pay your way into status, and monetize it. Further, influence is often a byproduct of status. Therefore, fundamentally speaking, it all starts with knowledge. As unicorn entrepreneur and Impact Theory founder Tom Bilyeu said: "Knowledge isn't power. Used knowledge is power."

The way we access and acquire knowledge these days is radically different from times past. Plus, the way we establish status and influence is also radically different from times past, thanks to social media platforms and the like. People can now establish an online presence at warp speed. It's important to consider what you do with your knowledge, status, and influence especially since it's faster and easier to acquire each.

These aspects of wealth are also incredibly important to consider in the age where the "company" takes on the archetype of an individual and the "individual" takes on the archetype of a company. Personal branding, naturally, invites us to analyze ourselves and what we present to the world. In this, there is a responsibility to model a meaningful life versus a superficial life. This idea is reflected in the Latin phrase *Praesis ut prosis re ut imperes*, which translates to "*lead in order to serve, not in order to rule*." The world is changed by the examples of others.

At this point, you may be thinking, where does power fold into all of this? We will discuss power, too, while highlighting the importance of personal power, which enables the accumulation of knowledge and unlocks the potential for status and influence, in order to serve. Along this thread, it's worth mentioning the movement away from the theatrics of power (the good ole peacock mentality) toward invisible, personal power that can be used to advance society forward in stealth mode.

"Bragging about yourself violates norms of modesty and politeness—and if you were really competent, your work would speak for itself."
—*Adam Grant*

 ## The Wealth of Time, Energy, and Experiences

Principle 4 (P4) emphasizes the parallel between investing money during economic cycles and investing time and energy throughout life. Often, both as an investor and as an individual, we seek the peaks. In other words, we seek the market highs and peak experiences, but the market lows and mundane moments deserve equal emphasis, too. A savvy investor knows how to optimize market dips, just the same as a savvy individual knows how to optimize mundane moments. Finding opportunity in both the ups and downs allows one to fully invest their time and energy, appreciating the totality of life. After all, time plus energy equals your life.

Time, many would say, is the most important asset we have. Miami's mayor, Francis Suarez, summarized it well: "the rarest asset we have is time … and the most important investment decision you will make in your life is not what you do with your money, it's what you do with your time." I heard these words at a pivotal time in my life when I was deciding whether to stay in Miami or move back to New York City. While my decision on where to live remained in suspension, it was Mayor Suarez's words that inspired me to stay in Miami. It was time to make a decision and forge forward, walking away from wasting time and energy in indecision.

"Trade money for time, not time for money. You're going to run out of time first."
—*Naval Ravikant*

The Wealth of Relationships, with Self and Others

Finally, Principle 5 (P5) explores the wealth of relationships, with self and others. The principle explores how we all desire intimate, meaningful relationships with family and friends; more so today than ever before, people are willing to set aside work to carve out time for their relationships, and thereby redefining their relational priorities in the process. This is a good thing, because interpersonal relationships are a necessary vehicle for personal growth. We're constantly revisiting, reimagining, and redefining who we are by virtue of our interactions with others, and vice versa. We're also reimagining who we interreact with, in the digital age, because we can now connect with others based on relevancy instead of just proximity. I firmly believe this is more profound than we currently realize.

That said, P5 also addresses the evolving value of relationships and the focus on surrounding yourself with people who inspire and improve you. It's okay to be selective with the company you keep. By surrounding yourself with people who inspire you, you expand your thinking and challenge your beliefs. Without others, there's no feedback loop, and we risk stagnation of self-evolution. It's also critical to consider relationship capital. A wealth of business relationships can lead to better career opportunities, and a wealth of personal relationships can lead to people being there for you in good times and in bad. As Margaret Walker said, "Friends and good manners will carry you where money won't go."

These 5 *Principles of Invisible Wealth* are distinct, stand-alone conversations, but they are also interrelated, coming together to embody the expanded concept of *wealth*.

Chapter 5
The Wealth of Money and Investment

Money is a resource that opens doors to rich potential. Money enables the attainment of security, freedom, choice, plus innovation, which is why it's so powerful. The more money we have, the more safety, flexibility, and optionality is available—broadly speaking—which then invites more opportunity for taking chances and seeking out new ventures. People invest money with the goal of gaining more of this resource, and the materials purchased with this gain.

While this book does over-index on the qualitative, intangible aspects of wealth, there is no denying that the quantitative, tangible aspects of wealth are a necessary part of the wealth discussion. After over a decade in private wealth management, I thoroughly understand the importance of financial wealth creation. As I'd say to my clients, money has the potential to enhance the most important things in life.

In this chapter, we'll delve into the interconnected relationship between money, investment, and wealth. This includes a journey through how we make, inherit, spend, save, and invest money these days, all of which have been influenced by technological innovations and societal shifts. Additionally, we will examine the broader societal implications of wealth creation. Let's begin.

The Relationship Between Money, Investment, and Wealth

Money has a powerful relationship with investment and wealth, because the three are interconnected. Money accumulated over and above your expenses and savings goals can be invested, putting your money to work; you work for your money, and then your money works for you. Money invested has the potential to outpace inflation and increase in value, thereby creating financial wealth. Additional moneys earned through investment returns can then be reinvested, furthering the potential for additional wealth creation. This is called compounding (more on this later). The dollars you earn are the seeds that lead to the full-grown money tree.

Money is foundational to wealth creation, which is why we'll explore all the ways we make, inherit, spend, save, and invest money these days. The way we interact with money is changing right before our eyes, and this change is largely due to technological innovations and cultural shifts. Further, there's no doubt that the way we interface with money and our relationship with money will continue to change, exponentially.

The bottom line is money matters, so let's talk about it—making it, inheriting it, spending it, saving it, and investing it, plus the societal implications of each.

Making Money

To spend, save, or invest money, we must first make (or inherit) it. The once dogmatic perspective of how to make money is evolving with time, so let's do a quick review of this evolution. Rewind the tape and look back at how the majority of people used to make money, it was through employment at a single company for much of their life. The company (employer) provided the individual (employee) with a sense of financial security in the form of a bi-weekly check, and thereafter, a healthy pension upon retirement. Gone are the days when people stay with the same company for the entirety of their professional careers. Over time, the decoupling of employer-employee loyalty began unraveling. In my mind, this inflection point started when employers stopped offering pension plans to their employees (beginning in the 1980s).[1] Then came the proliferation of the internet, which expanded employment opportunities in ways previously unthinkable.

The once reliable and expected career path of working for one employer for a lifetime, earning a pension, and then settling into retirement is a relic of the past. Retirement funding is now the responsibility of the individual employee, and loyalty between employers and employees has gradually faded. This morphing of loyalties—in both directions—opened the door for people to move from one organization to the next or to start a company of their own. Play the tape forward and gaps in a résumés are now more accepted, even celebrated, as it demonstrates a willingness to take risks to pursue a bigger opportunity and to increase earning potential. Side hustles and entrepreneurship are the new norms—and so is having multiple streams of income.

Multiple Streams of Income

Having multiple streams of income is a smart way to increase your cash flow, thereby increasing the amount of money you have. There are many ways to set up multiple streams of income, some of which evolved with time, the economy, technological advancement, and human ingenuity. New avenues for income generation are coming online, both literally and figuratively. Generally speaking, there are three categories of income: *active income, passive income*, and *investment/portfolio income*. Let's quickly define each:

1. *Active income* is the income earned through a job that you diligently participate in.
2. *Passive income* is the income earned through little participation.
3. *Investment income* is the income earned from your investment portfolio, in the form of interest, dividends, and capital gains.

The most common stream of income was, and remains, active income. This is income earned from salaried employment: people receiving pay for their active involvement in (specialized) work tasks. Passive income and investment income are the next most common types of income streams. Passive income is the income earned through little participation; for example, rental income from a property owned and rented out to another. Although one owns the property and may have to care for it, there's very little active involvement once it's rented out to another party. Investment income is the income you earn from your investment portfolio; for example, Apple stock pays a dividend to their investors, four times a year (quarterly). Typically, people diversify their investment portfolio to gain exposure to different asset classes and sectors. This is a great way to manage investment risk. And now, people are diversifying the way in which they bring in income just the same as they diversify their investment portfolio. This is a great way to manage income risk.

Side hustles are remarkably common nowadays, providing additional streams of income into the wallets of many. In 2022, one in three Americans had a side hustle, and two-thirds of these people said they loved their side hustle.[2] These are meaningful numbers and sentiments. About 50% of millennials have a side hustle, while 70% of Gen Z's have a side hustle. Lots of people are doing what they love, all the while contributing value to the economy; specifically, $2.58 trillion worth of value.[3] These dollars are funneling through gig economy powerhouses such as Airbnb, Uber, TaskRabbit, and Etsy. Workers are leveraging these new ecosystems and influencing the economy, capitalizing on cultural shifts. The shift toward multiple streams of income (supported by entrepreneurial spirit animals and digital transformations) is shape-shifting the character of the economy.

The Creator Economy + Web3

Speaking of the character of the economy, creatives are influencing the characteristics of commerce and economies. The creator economy is the segment of the "economy empowering people who are monetizing their content, goods and services online by leveraging their own creativity, talents and passions."[4] Creators use technology, more specifically software platforms, to power and actualize their creations. Think software platforms such as: YouTube, TikTok, Instagram, Facebook, Substack, and Patreon (which are all alternatives to traditional media).[5] As a result, creators are providing value to the world, and monetizing it. People create content and distribute it through these platforms. More than 165 million creators joined the creator economy between 2020 and 2022, for a total of 303 million creators worldwide.[6] Millennials represent 42%

of the creator economy, while Gen Z's represent 14%.[7] In 2022, the creator economy generated $104 billion of value.[8] About 48% of creators are motivated by freedom of expression.[9] There's a shift from stiff, unoriginal work to creative, original work.

This new economic trend is reshaping society; *The Artist's Way* (a nod to the book by Julia Cameron). This is a huge unlock. On one side of the coin, we have creators providing value, doing what they love, and making money for it. On the other side of the coin, we have consumers receiving value, consuming what they want, and enriching themselves in the process. Essentially, this is peer-to-peer education and entertainment. Creators are sharing their wherewithal, on demand, with consumers who are interested in their content. This content has the potential for reaching eyes and ears that otherwise would not be available, which is particularly alluring to our increasingly autodidactic society. This trend will have huge implications in the shifting of economies and culture.

While there are many creators making lots of money in the limelight, there is also a dark side to the current structure of this industry. The dark side is that creators typically walk away with little (or no) monetary gain for their creations; instead, the value created ends up lining the pockets of the platforms distributing the content. However, technological innovation may be the antidote—in the form of Web3. You may be asking what is Web3? And you're not alone. The term *Web3* only entered our lexicon in 2014 (when Ethereum co-founder Gavin Wood coined it). But it wasn't until 2021 that this concept started getting off the ground.[10] That said, we are in the nascent stages of conceptualizing, let alone actualizing, the potential of Web3.

Web3 stands to unlock more monetary value for creators, thereby elevating the creator economy. Here's why: Web3 is expected to be the third iteration, or generation, of the World Wide Web. This third generation of the web is powered by blockchain technology, and places a strong emphasis on being open, decentralized, and trustable.[11] Blockchain will enable peer-to-peer (in this context, creators to consumers) interaction without the need for an intermediary, distributive platform. Meaning more money into the pockets of the creatives, all the while retaining 100% ownership of their data. Elevating the creator economy will inspire more content creation, without ad-driven monetization strategies (on centralized platforms).[12] These sentiments and themes are similar to those we saw with Bitcoin, with the dissolving of the intermediary. Web3 could revolutionize work (just the same as Web1 and Web2 did previously). In which case, the way we make money will continue evolving, and quickly. Therefore, the future of wealth and the future of the internet (Web3) are inherently interconnected. And this is only the beginning.

Inheriting Money

Speaking of the next generation, I'd be remiss not to mention the potential of acquiring wealth through inheritance. Especially because, and as we already know, millennials are expected to inherit $84 trillion from their baby boomer parents by 2045.[13] A generational wealth transfer is underway. In other words, wealth that spans multiple generations. Regardless of whether you make your own money or inherit money, it's still purchasing power in your pocket.

Spending Money

Money acts as a reflection of what we value. What we value and prioritize ultimately drives *how* we make money, and *what* we spend money on. As the saying goes, "show me your receipts, and I'll show you what you value," although, these days, many receipts are electronic rather than strips of white paper. Digital receipts are a prime example of the evolving ways we interface with money (i.e., how we make payments) thanks to innovative technologies.

At the beginning of this chapter, I presented a core belief—the belief that money has the potential to enhance the most important things in life. For example, spending money on your health has the ability to dramatically enhance your quality of life. Similarly, spending money on experiences with loved ones is a consequential enhancement, too. Money well spent is additive, whereas money poorly spent is detractive to one's life. This is where values-based spending steps into our wealth journey. Values-based spending means spending on things that are in alignment with your values; reflecting what's most important to you. It's a personalized approach to spending. Sometimes this might mean right-sizing your spending habits, but it doesn't have to. This type of orientation around spending certainly doesn't mean forgoing things you enjoy—by all means, buy what makes you happy and enriches your life. After all, the ability to spend money (on x, y, and z) is a great motivator for making money.

In Chapter 2, we saw that millennials (and other generations, of course) are generally more interested in values-based spending, and both businesses and money managers are taking notice. Consumers are voting with their wallets and showcasing a preference for spending on services over goods, or intangibles over tangibles. We're witnessing a shift away from spending on tangible things (materialism) and toward spending on intangibles (minimalism). We're valuing more space than more stuff. Plus, while tangible things (like cars) tend to depreciate over time, intangibles (like experiences) tend to hold their value, and even compound with time. Take the experience of travel. Travel gives one invaluable perspective, cultural exposure, and broadening of viewpoints, all of which are beneficial.

> *"A man is rich in proportion to the number of things he can afford to let alone."*
> —*Henry David Thoreau*

Regardless of what you spend your money on, finding and buying what you want is much easier and efficient these days. Search, select, purchase, and receive almost anything you want from the comfort of your own home. And recieve, in a matter of minutes, hours, or at most - a few days. Clearly, these technological advancements in the e-commerce and the payments space are incredibly influential on our spending habits. The most common example of this is the proliferation of Amazon, but let's not forget all the brands and companies that now have online stores (perhaps in addition to brick-and-mortar stores). We now have the ability to buy what we need, with a few simple keystrokes, all the while saving time on travel to and from a store.

The way in which we transact to spend money has changed, too—think PayPal, Venmo, and digital wallets like Apple Pay. Apple Pay uses near-field communication, otherwise known as tap-to-pay, which enables you to put your phone *near* the checkout kiosk, and like magic, payment is made. Near-field communication is also the technology responsible for the ability to wave your card over a subway or bus turnstile, paying and granting access.[14] There are also digital wallets for people who want to transact in cryptocurrencies, like Coinbase and Metamask. Retailers such as Home Depot, Shopify, and Microsoft all accept bitcoin.[15] The barriers to shopping and paying are nearly eradicated. What we see reflected back to us is the stark change in the way we interface with invisible money; we reimagined the payments system. In 2020, cash was used in only 11.4% of transactions.[16]

But what are we to do with all the money that we don't spend? Save it and invest it.

Saving Money

Saving money implies forgoing the purchasing of visible things, keeping your money invisible to the outside world.

Traditionally, financial advisors suggest having six months' worth of expenses saved in cash, before investing excess money. Some people opt for more or less cash on hand, depending on their annual income, annual expenses, risk tolerance, and overall financial goals. By the way, it's interesting to see how idioms such as "cash on hand" remain prevalent in society when it's no longer physical dollars in our wallet but a swipe of a credit card in a digital transaction. This is another example of the evolving meaning of words and idioms.

Having savings (aka cash on hand) provides peace of mind, because it creates a safety cushion if your income (whether it be active, passive, or investment income) unexpectedly decreases or expenses increase. Saved monies are earmarked for times of need due to unforeseen or one-off changes in financial circumstances. For this reason, the nature of your work—in other words, the regularity and predictability of your income (streams)—should be taken into consideration when determining how much money to keep in your rainy-day fund. Intuitively, early-stage entrepreneurs tend to have more variability in income, therefore their cash cushion might be bigger. Conversely, someone with a more predictable paycheck may not need quite as much cash on hand. Either way, the amount of money that gives you peace of mind is unique to you.

Once a comfortable cash cushion is in place, then the real wealth journey begins.

Investing Money

Sitting comfortably on top of your cash cushion is a great place to start your wealth creation journey. Saving money is a productive step in the wealth creation process, but the real lift comes from investing your money for growth purposes. The best way to grow your money is by keeping it invested or, in other words, invisible. This section places a magnifying glass on the ever-evolving relationship between money, investment, and wealth. The relationship between money and wealth has a lot to do with access to investment information and investment opportunities; the more information and opportunity you have to invest your money, the higher the likelihood for meaningful wealth creation.

Being invested means putting your money to work behind the scenes, as it remains invisible to the outside world. The current paradigm and societal shifts—away from materialism—support and encourage the transition from visible wealth to invisible wealth.

The question then becomes: what and how should you invest your money in such a dynamic investment landscape? This is an internal exploration first, before it's an external exploration—meaning the answer is rooted in a handful of considerations (which a financial advisor would be happy to walk you through). This means considering your annual income, your annual expenses, your investment risk tolerance, and your overall financial goals in the long-term and short-term. The income consideration is particularly interesting given the topics discussed, like the Great Migration, the Great Resignation, and the Great Restructuring—translating into more unconventional work. After addressing these considerations, the exploration shifts externally to the *what* and the *how* of investing. One thing is for sure, a diversified investment portfolio is a must. The what, how, and why of what we invest in has changed from years past. While the next bit is by no means a comprehensive deep dive into investing, it does illuminate the macro shifts in landscape.

Investing Before the Internet

Before the internet, people typically invested in public markets with the help of a stockbroker. Public market investment refers to the buying of equity or debt of a publicly owned company (versus a privately owned company). Public markets were (and remain) accessible through investing in individual stocks, bonds, mutual funds, or exchange-traded funds through a stockbroker. By definition, a broker is an intermediary. Logistically, a phone call to your broker was the primary way to invest. The broker would provide you with some level of investment information and advice, and then execute the investment transaction—for a price. For perspective, a full-service broker could charge 2.5% commission on a trade.[17] Want to know how an investment was performing a month later? Call your stockbroker. There was total reliance on the intermediary, and it would cost you.

Before the internet, people faced barriers to investing, in the form of lack of information, transparency, and access, plus financial barriers in the form of high commission costs. But the internet changed all of this by changing the way we interface with the investment ecosystem, and it changed the investment ecosystem itself. The public stock market met online brokerage services for retail investors in 1992—thanks to E*TRADE.[18]

Retail Revolution

Today, people invest in public markets through online brokers like E*TRADE or my former employer, Fidelity, but also newcomers like Robinhood—to buy and sell public securities. Nowadays, there are $0 commission brokerage firms. This is an example of how technology enables (commission) fee compression. Additionally, online brokers now provide troves of investment information and you can execute investment transactions yourself (if you have a brokerage account). Or, if you prefer, you can hire a financial advisor to provide investment advice and execution. The option is yours.

For these reasons, people are flocking to online brokers—finding the power to invest in their own hands. "In January 2021 alone, roughly six million Americans downloaded a retail brokerage trading app, joining well over

10 million Americans who opened up a new brokerage account in 2020."[19] Power in numbers; the rise of the retail investor—the retail revolution. As Deloitte put it, "A new breed of investor, empowered by new platforms." There's a monumental increase in the "do it yourself" investor, who feels empowered and equipped with access to information and online trading tools. This thematically aligns with the ethos of entrepreneurs, in the sense that people are taking matters into their own hands—when it comes to both making money and investing money.

Public and Private Markets

Let's twirl our attention from public markets to private markets. Private markets used to be, well, more private—or, for the sake of staying on brand here—invisible. Although, nowadays, private markets are at the forefront of many investment discussions and portfolio returns.

Private market investment refers to the buying of equity or debt of a privately owned company (versus a publicly owned company). Private markets are accessible through private equity funds, hedge funds, private debt, and venture capital funds. Private market investments are also referred to as "alternative" investments, meaning they are an alternative to the traditional, public market investments. One key distinction between public and private markets is alternative, private markets are less regulated than traditional, public markets. Despite less regulation, private markets attract lots of money. While 10 million Americans opened up new brokerage accounts in 2020, for purposes of investing in the public markets, the private markets reached an all time fundraising high in 2021.[20] The private markets attracted nearly $1.2 trillion in 2021, globally.[21] According to Preqin's *The Future of Alternatives* report, global alternative assets are likely to surpass $14 trillion by 2023.[22] The private, alternative, non-traditional market is becoming less private, alternative, and non-traditional. There are many factors at play here, but for the scope of our conversation—which focuses on the investment of money for wealth creation—let's look to the return profiles of keeping your savings in cash, investing it in the public markets, and investing it in the private markets.

With a comfortable cash cushion in place, the real wealth journey begins. For sake of conversation, assume you have $100,000 earmarked for investment. The year is 2000, and you don't plan on touching this money until 2021. You're considering: leaving your money in cash, investing in public equities, or investing in private equity. First, if you kept your money in cash, you'd have $100,000 in 2021[23]. Second, if you invested into public equities, you'd have $406,005 in 2021[24]. Third, if you invested into private equity, you'd have $894,917 in 2021. Why? Because public equities returned 6.9% from 2000 through 2021[25], and private equity returned 11%[26] during this same timeframe. To be clear, there are considerations we aren't discussing like risks, fees, inflation, return variability, compounding frequency, taxes, and liquidity, but the point is higher returns result in higher wealth creation. Investing is such an important part of the wealth journey. The sub-point is, private markets tend to have higher returns, which is why they're so attractive to investors (when one's investor profile supports).

The reason I used the $100,000 investment amount, over a 21-year time horizon is to illustrate that private investments often require significant amounts of money and time. (Two disclaimers. First, private investment structures, and therefore commitment amounts, vary widely. Two, the timeframe isn't representative of the average private investment, but rather the timeframe we have clean data on. Long term data is better than short term data. Plus, it supports the notion of long-term investing.) Private investments are typically reserved for institutional and high-net worth (aka accredited) investors. An accredited investor is someone who has a net worth over $1 million (excluding primary residence), or makes over $200,000 a year or satisfies certain professional criteria.[27] The intention of this federal regulation is to limit alternatives to people with the means or sophistication to take on more risk.[28]

But access to the private investment world is changing: the public is gaining more access to privates.

The Democratization of Wealth

There's incredible emphasis on the "democratization of wealth," which aims at providing more people with more access to investment information and investment opportunity (both in public and private markets). Ultimately, this enables wealth creation for more people. The demand for the democratization of wealth has opened the door for many investors to access wealth-generating investment opportunities. How? Through regulatory changes and financial innovations. For instance, in 2020, the SEC expanded the definition of an "accredited investor," allowing more people to qualify for this investor status.[29] As a result, more people can now access alternative investments. Plus, new financial innovations are coming to market and reimagining and redefining the traditional approach to investment.

Digitization and democratization go hand-in-hand. On the public market side of the coin, we see the Robinhood's of the world on a mission "to democratize finance for all." Robinhood democratizes finance by offering free investment information, commission-free trading, and fractional share trading. This is productive because it provides free investment education, plus lower fees barriers to entry for retail investors. Wealthfront is another example of a fintech entity leveraging digitization for the democratization of wealth. Wealthfront is a "robo-advisor," which means it's a digital financial advisor. The Wealthfront platform walks you through an array of questions to determine your investment profile, risk tolerance, financial goals, and time horizon. From there, the digital software builds a diversified portfolio based on your answers—all this, for a fraction of the cost of traditional wealth managers. Technology is scaling financial sophistication, and it's doing so in an approachable and affordable way. This is a win for the retail investor.

One final example, under the democratization of wealth umbrella, is Ellevest. Ellevest, co-founded by Sallie Krawcheck, is a "women-first financial company" that's on a mission to get more money into the hands of women.[30] They offer financial advisory services, coaching, worksheets, workshops, and access to a magazine full of personal finance insights—all tailored to support women on their wealth creation journey. Much needed, and very empowering.

On the private market side of the coin, we see new entrants, such as Titan, who are democratizing access to portfolio management as well as access to private markets to retail investors. Titan is an online brokerage and "investment platform, building a personalized private wealth experience for all."[31] In September 2022, they announced that retail investors can now allocate into private funds managed by alternative investment giants Apollo Global Management and the Carlyle Group.[32] Also in September 2022, Titan announced its exclusive partnership with Cathie Wood's ARK Invest, to allow retail investors to invest in ARK's Venture Capital Fund— for as little as $500.[33] These are big developments for the democratization of wealth. We'll continue seeing investment opportunities expand for all types of investors. An Ernst & Young study showed that 73% of asset managers believe non-accredited investors should receive access to invest in private funds, in order to increase their portfolio diversification and participate in potentially higher returns.[34] These are game-changing investment innovations, unlocking new doors to wealth creation.

These are a few investment innovations attempting to bridge the wealth gap—for a more sustainable, financial future for all.

Sustainable Investing

Speaking of a sustainable financial future for all, investors are increasingly interested in both the value (quantitative) and values (qualitative) of an investment. In other words, investor due diligence is extending beyond the tangible and into the realms of the intangible. Naturally, the investment return profile is important, but so are investment themes, specifically environmental, social, and governance—colloquially known as "ESG". ESG investing is a concept and a framework for considering non-financial factors when measuring the viability of an investment. Said differently, ESG investing is a form of sustainable investing that considers environmental, social, and/or governance elements when evaluating an investment opportunity.[35] Let's drill down a little further.

What type of considerations fall into each of these three ESG buckets? First, environmental considerations include carbon emissions, air and water pollution, and waste management. Second, social considerations include data security, employee diversity, and customer satisfaction. Third, governance considerations include diversity of board members, executive pay, political contributions, and lobbying.[36]

The ESG commitments of a company are important investment consideration for four reasons: financial strength, competitive positioning, innovative strategy, and perception or corporate reputation.[37] Each of these have the potential to reduce investment risk and increase investment return. These benefits extend beyond the investor, and to all the stakeholders as well—employees, consumers, and society. For example, investing in a company dedicated to reducing their carbon footprint is valuable to the investor, and society at large.

As the economic landscape becomes more dynamic, so, too, our investment decisions. There's a conversation going on between investors and investment opportunities determining which factors are of utmost importance when it comes to investing. The message is loud and clear from the values-based, millennial generation—but also from most other investors too. There is collective interest and demand for socially responsible investments. This is an integral component of the *new wealth paradigm*.

Now for the numbers, to underscore how this holistic approach to investing is shifting the investment landscape in a meaningful way. As of December 2021, assets under management in exchange-traded ESG funds—globally—totaled more than $2.7 trillion.[38] In 2021, alone, over $500 billion flowed into ESG funds from investors.[39] It's projected that ESG mandated investments will make up half of all professionally managed assets, worldwide, by 2024.[40] Half! By 2024! The real focus now is ensuring companies and businesses stay true to the investment mandate and ethos.

Blockchain and Digital Assets

Continuing on the theme of tech innovations and societal shifts, let's fold blockchain technology back into the conversation. Blockchain will play a major role in the democratization of wealth and sustainable investing. Understanding blockchain technology, cryptography and cryptocurrency is helpful for considering and appreciating this conclusive statement.

What Is Blockchain Technology?

Here are the building blocks of blockchain technology, plus cryptography and cryptocurrency.

Blockchain technology was first introduced in 2008 in the Bitcoin white paper (see Chapter 1). Elementally, blockchain is a peer-to-peer network that sits on top of the internet.[41] The Blockchain Research Institute provides a great definition for this technology: "A blockchain is a distributed software network that functions both as a digital ledger and a mechanism enabling the secure transfer of assets without an intermediary. Just as the internet is a technology that facilitates the digital flow of information, blockchain is a technology that facilitates the digital exchange of units of value."[42] Bitcoin and cryptocurrencies included.

To understand what cryptocurrencies are, we must first understand what cryptography is. The first known use of cryptography was in 1900 BCE, which makes a lot of sense when you consider what cryptography is. Cryptography is simply the securing of communication from those who are not intended to receive the communication.[43] This can be achieved through code. Interestingly enough, "crypto" comes from the Greek word "kruptos," which means "hidden." Hidden is inherently *invisible*.

Cryptocurrencies are tradable digital assets built on blockchain technology that use cryptography to control the creation of coins and to verify transactions.[44] Cryptocurrencies are decentralized assets, which are key components of decentralized finance (commonly referred to as "DeFi"). Decentralized finance is a financial system powered by individuals rather than a central authority. Many believe this technology will revolutionize traditional finance because it offers a fundamentally new way for commerce and society to self-organize. It's even been said that the internet democratized knowledge, and blockchain will democratize wealth.[45]

We're seeing a society of values emerge with the internet of value, in tandem.

Decentralized Finance (DeFi)

With an understanding for blockchain technology, cryptography and cryptocurrency, let's explore two practical use cases. Democratize wealth by providing the technological infrastructure for a decentralized financial ecosystem. Decentralized finance offers an alternative to traditional, centralized finance services by dissolving the need for intermediaries and centralized trust mechanisms. DeFi allows people to conduct peer-to-peer financial transactions through technology (versus a brokerage firm, for example).[46] The technology used in these peer-to-peer transactions are enabled by smart contracts on a blockchain. These smart contracts are smart; so, they automatically execute according to the terms of the contract (or agreement), in a trustworthy way.[47] Smart contracts are basically conditions programmed into the blockchain; if x then y. Furthermore, this is the financial architecture that makes Web3's vision of a decentralized (creator) economy possible. The bottom line is DeFi represents the potential for: peer-to-peer transactions, trust via technology, lower fees, faster transactions, and more transparency when compared to traditional financial systems. This translates into the opportunity to "bank the unbanked" by providing digital wallets to those who cannot establish a bank account (through an intermediary). This is a powerful way to activate and increase financial inclusion.

Here is a practical example of DeFi; of blockchain technology decentralizing finance and democratizing wealth. In September 2022, KKR, a behemoth private equity firm, broadened access to one of their funds through digital ownership on blockchain. Said differently, KKR tokenized a portion of one of their funds, on a blockchain, granting access to investors for a fraction of the money typically required to invest. Just as investors can buy fractional shares in public equity through Robinhood, KKR is providing a way for investors (qualified purchasers) to buy fractional shares in private equity. The fractionalization of investments (using blockchain technology) is lowering the investment commitment required; in this case, to $20,000. As we know, historically, investment into private markets has been reserved for those with very deep pockets. This is changing. KKR, in partnership with Securitize (a digital assets securities firm), is solving for this "by enabling technology to deliver lower investment minimums, improved digital investor onboarding and compliance protocols, and increased potential for liquidity through a regulated alternative trading system."[48] Further, Securitize CEO Carlos Domingo says, "This new fund is an important step toward democratizing access to private equity investments by delivering more efficient access to institutional quality products." While $20,000 is still a hefty investment commitment, this is, indeed, a step in the right direction.

Additionally, blockchain technology can support sustainable investing considerations. A practical example is the use of blockchain in ethical sourcing and supply chain transparency, because of the technology's trustworthy, transparent, and traceable nature. Blockchain provides the technological infrastructure to record the origin and transactions of goods along the supply chain, providing reliable, indisputable, and accountable insight into the origins and whereabouts of goods every step of the way. This applies to everything from coffee beans to computer chips. Blockchain's trustworthy nature is rooted in the fact that we are trusting decentralized technology rather than a centralized intermediary to manage and report on ESG considerations. Plus, blockchain provides transparency and traceability because it's a digital, immutable ledger. This ledger can be viewed by consumers, investors, and regulators interested in the sourcing and supply chain metrics of a particular good. Therefore, blockchain provides a clear pathway for values-based companies to build, manage, and report on their ESG commitments.[49]

As previously mentioned, we now have a ripe opportunity to reimagine and redefine wealth because so much of what we value, both individually and collectively, is changing. Technological advancements and societal shifts are unlocking the potential for a decentralized financial system. Blockchain provides the foundation for the next era of finance, powered by the quest for personal sovereignty, financial inclusion, trust, and transparency. This shift values both the quantitative and qualitative aspects of the economy, tethering personal finance to personal philosophy. As a consequence, the velocity of adoption is something we haven't seen before. Blockchain and crypto are shattering old paradigms of value and making meaningful changes to the world of finance and therefore, wealth. Needless to say, the next decade will be transformative and mind-bending.

The main takeaway here is that there are many ways to approach investing and keeping your money invisible to create wealth (instead of leaving excess money in cash, which loses purchasing power over time due to inflation). Investing, and keeping your money invested, increases your potential for exponential growth due to compounding. Compounding interest is the money you earn from your investment's interest. We'll see in the next segment of this chapter why compounding is not only beneficial for the individual account holder, but also society as a whole. After all, there's a reason Albert Einstein called it "the eighth wonder of the world".

Societal Implications of Wealth Creation

Keeping your money invested gives it the potential to grow in value and to compound. Compounding interest is the money you earn from your investment's interest, which is incredibly powerful for the account holder and is a motivator for investing money in the first place. This is a well-considered and discussed concept. What we don't often consider and discuss are the beneficial implications of compounding interest for those beyond the account holder. In other words, how one person's ability to increase the value of their money has compounding effects for society.

Not only does the account holder benefit from the exponential growth that comes with compounding interest, but perhaps others do too—truly drawing on compounding *interests*, by many (versus one). It is in the individual account owner's interest *and* society's interest to have money growing at exponential rates, because once the account owner acquires enough wealth for themselves, then they are more inclined to share their wealth with others. This could be with loved ones or loved causes like a charity, or a socially responsible investment. Exponential wealth has the potential to support a multitude of interests, both in a vertical framework (grandparents, parents, kids, grandkids) and in a horizontal framework (community, state, country, world). For example, the Great Wealth Transfer is shifting money from the hands of boomers to milennials. Plus, financial wealth allows one to take on more risks in the arena of entrepreneurship and innovation—something we all stand to benefit from. By accumulating wealth, one is able to reduce the consequences of taking risks and this allows for more innovation, which is beneficial on an individual level and a societal level.

It's worth pulling forward the etymological pearls of insight we discovered in Chapter 1, which showed us that the definition of wealth started as a noun relating to the individual. Thereafter, the term expanded conceptual reach to the community. This supports the premise that wealth relates to the individual first, and then has the potential to expand to society.

Another benefit, or application, of compounding *interests* beyond the account holder is the concept of "voting with your wallet." Let's consider what "voting with your wallet" means. This saying represents the spending or investing of money in ways that align with your values. When we support brands, stores, movements, or investments that are in alignment with our values, we provide the financial fuel to support their success. What we appreciate, appreciates. Here's an example: let's assume it's really important for you to support local farmers and to eat organic food. In this case, you decide to purchase organic food from the local farmers market to support and sustain their business. As a result, you are not buying conventional apples from a large supermarket in town. This creates an inherent feedback loop, by signaling to the large supermarket that you are not interested in their conventional apples, thereby influencing the supply/demand dynamics. One key point here is that local, organic foods tend to be more expensive than a bundle of conventional apples. Therefore, those with more wealth are in a stronger position to vote with their wallets and influence society in a positive way. The more people voting with their wallet and demanding organic food (for example), the higher the aggregate demand, thereby ultimately reducing cost (for all). (This hypothetical assumes an increase in farmers converting to organic farming over time, and with production costs decreasing.)

There's no denying that money is powerful; it will always be a resource that enables the attainment of security, freedom, choice, and innovation. Plus, money has the potential to enhance the most important things in life. For this reason, the more people who make, inherit, save, and invest their money with the potential for exponential growth, the better, because of the compounding *interests* at play. We all reap the rewards of the democratization and widespread access to wealth creation.

"The only wealth which you will keep is the wealth you have given away."
—*Marcus Aurelius*

Chapter 6
The Wealth of Health and Quality of Life

In the previous chapter, we talked about money: making, inheriting, spending, saving, and investing it, plus the remarkable shifts influencing each. Money certainly has the potential to enhance the most important things in life, but only when health is accounted for. Health is the foundation on which all else is built.

With this in mind, let's explore the second *Principle of Invisible Wealth* (P2). But beforehand, I'll preface with saying this is where the conversation starts over-indexing on the qualitative aspects of wealth. The first principle focuses on personal finance, whereas the second principle focuses on personal health. We'll explore the fundamentally familiar concept of "health is wealth" through a refreshed lens, inviting us to reimagine and redefine health and quality of life.

The Relationship Between Health, Quality of Life, and Wealth

Speaking of definitions, in Chapter 1 we started the exploration of wealth with its etymological origins; specifically, how the word "wealth" was born from "*wele*".

The etymology of *wealth* as a noun:

Mid 13-c., "happiness," also "prosperity in abundance of possessions or riches," from Middle English *wele* "well-being" (see weal (n.1)) on analogy of health.[1]

The etymology of "weal":

"well-being," Old English wela "wealth," in late Old English also "welfare, well-being," from West Germanic *welon-, from PIE root *wel- (2) "to wish, will" (see will (v)). Related to well (adv.)[2]

This reveals the fact that wealth found its definitional roots in health and well-being. This is true in an etymological sense, and true in a practical sense. Health, practically speaking, is foundational to both creating wealth and enjoying wealth. Consider this. First, our mind, body, and spirit must be healthy to make money, which can then be invested for wealth creation purposes. Therefore, we must be healthy to enjoy the fruits of our labor and investment, thereby contributing to the quality of our lives.

The health of an individual's income relies on the health of the economy. The health of the economy relies on the health of the individual. And the health of the individual relies on the health of their income. Full circle.

Wealth of Health: The Foundation on Which All Else Is Built

"When health is absent, wisdom cannot reveal itself, art cannot manifest, strength cannot fight, wealth becomes useless, and intelligence cannot be applied."

—*Herophilus*

Health is foundational to the other *Principles of Invisible Wealth*, which are: money and investment; knowledge, status, and influence; time, energy, and experiences; plus, relationships with self and others. Let's do an examination, so to speak, into how health is the backbone of each principle.

First, health is necessary to make money, because it enables you to perform the work at hand. There are "sick days" for a reason; you don't want to work when you're not feeling well, and your employer doesn't want you to work when you're not feeling well either, because you're bound to be less productive. We do our best work, whether it be as a construction worker or a software engineer, when you're healthy. There are plenty of data to support this. The data show a positive correlation between health and financial wealth: the healthier you are, the wealthier you can be, and the wealthier you are, the healthier you can be. Here are some numbers for my analytical friends: 22.8% of people making less than $35,000 per year reported they are in fair or poor health, whereas a mere 5.6% of people making more than $100,000 per year reported they are in fair or poor health. This is from a study done in 2015.[3]

> *"Healthy citizens are the greatest asset any country can have."*
> —*Winston Churchill*

Second, health is necessary for accumulating and using knowledge, status, and influence. The accumulation of knowledge requires the exercising of the mind. When you're unable to exercise your mind—due to stress, fatigue, or any other health deficiency—you're unable to accumulate and use knowledge. With health intact, using knowledge often supports the acquisition of status and influence within society. Sharing knowledge, and using your status and influence for the benefit of those around you, is incredibly important for the integrity of society. Honorable use of knowledge, status, and influence is beneficial, both professionally and personally.

Third, health is inherently tied to time, energy, and experiences. With health comes increased longevity, vitality, and happiness. While it might take time and energy to attain and maintain optimal health, your return on investment is rewarded. Consider this: the Department of Health and Human Services (HHS) recommends that American adults exercise moderately for 150–300 minutes per week, or vigorously for 75–150 minutes per week. People who exercise above the recommended thresholds are 80% more likely to live longer.[4] Also, the healthier you are, the more energetic you are, thereby enhancing your zest for life. Energy is your lifeforce, fueling all that you do in life; the amount of vigor you bring to work and play. The food you eat, the sleep you get, and the exercise you do all relate to the energy you can give to yourself and others.

And fourth, speaking of self, health strongly impacts the quality of your relationship with your inner self. Your relationship with self is made up of the physical, mental, and spiritual. This symbiotic relationship between health and self influences soundess of body, mind, and spirit. When one is right with oneself, it serves as a foundation for building strong relationships with others. Human connection is essential. It's a source of happiness, which supports health.

Based on these factors it's easy to understand how the 5 *Principles of Invisible Wealth* coalesce around health: health impacts our ability to make money and therefore our ability to create financial wealth. Once longevity runs its course, wealth can then be left to loved ones and loved causes— charity and philanthropy. Health also impacts our ability to accumulate knowledge, status, and influence, to then share with friends, family, and colleagues. And, of course, we must have the time and energy to share these gifts with those around us; to fully enjoy the experience of life. Ultimately, everything is connected.

From this, it's clear why health is wealth—in an etymological sense, and in a practical sense.

What Is Health?

Revisiting, reimaging, and redefining wealth includes doing so for the definition of health, too. It's worth exercising and strengthening your concept of health, identifying what optimal health means for you, especially because health and the other *Principles of Invisible Wealth* are so intimately connected. Let's delve into the hows and whys for optimal physical, mental, and spiritual health. On a micro level, technology (ex: Oura ring) is helping to optimize health by providing visibility into the invisible markers of health. On a macro level, technology is enabling the democratization of health, just the same as it's doing for the democratization of (financial) wealth. Above all else, the intention of this principle is to highlight the grand scope and value of health.

Physical Health

When we think of health, we typically think of physical, visible health; this is the antiquated health narrative. This outdated concept of health typically considers that which we can see. It's easy to "see" when our health is off by simply looking in the mirror: body weight, clarity of skin, brightness of eyes, and other superficial changes. But our physical health is often a reflection of what's going on where we cannot "see." Physical ailments, unless we're talking scrapes and bruises, are often the manifestation of the unseen. Now, technological advancements (otherwise known as health-tech) are progressing both the visible and invisible realms of health.

Technological advancements are bringing visibility to the invisible attributes of physical health. Here are some relatable examples. A few months into the pandemic, I bought an Apple Watch, but I didn't buy it to tell me the time; rather, I bought it to monitor my blood oxygen level. There's no way I (or anyone else) could "see" my blood oxygen level without the help of the Apple Watch (which is considered wearable technology). Another relatable example is the Oura Ring, which is also a wearable providing visibility into the invisible. Over brunch, a friend showed me her Oura Ring analytics while scrolling through the sleek user interface on her phone. We could see all the biometric data the ring collected, which was organized in a fun and visually informative way. It's mindblowing how much information is now at our fingertips (sourced from our fingers). But like all types of information, it's what you do with it that really matters. This biometric data can inform how we structure our days (how we eat, sleep, and exercise), in order to optimize our health. In other words, we can use quantitative data to make qualitative changes.

Consistent health monitoring and data streaming enhances the ability to personalize and customize health regimes. My Apple Watch shows me tons of personalized and customized information. For example, it tells me how many calories I burn exercising in the morning. Personalization. And it also tells me what the current UV index is here in Miami. Customization. Melding these two together, the UV index influences when I exercise outside, because I try to avoid peak UV times. Sunscreen is helpful, but not when it's dripping off my skin. My friend's Oura Ring gives her a sleep score each day, after measuring the previous night's rest. The ring measures metrics like REM sleep and nightly heart rate. Based on this information, she wakes up to a sleep score that influences how she might structure her day. A 90% sleep score means heading to the gym and taking on those heavy weights. A 65% sleep score means taking it easy and leaving the heavy lifting for another day.

This leads me to the point that managing health is behavioral; behaviors that technology can influence and support. Digital natives (i.e., millennials) are most inclined to buy and use wearables to measure and inform their daily health decisions. Millennials are a subset of consumers who really value personalized health. But regardless of how much quantitative data you have, qualitative behavioral changes are hard, which is why wearables and health apps are implementing the power of gaming. Healthcare gamification means applying gaming principles, gaming design, and gaming mechanics to improve the health of the user.[5] Health is much more than just avoiding the flu these days. A Goldman Sachs report captures this perfectly: "Defining Healthy. For millennials, "healthy" doesn't just mean "not sick." It's a daily commitment to eating right and exercising."[6] Needless to say, everyone is reimaging their health practices, especially since the onset of the pandemic. During the pandemic, I researched which vitamins were best to prevent contracting the virus. I bought all the vitamins and lined the jars along my countertop, like a row of toy soldiers willing and able to combat the bad guys.

In addition to wearables and health apps, advancements in health-tech extend beyond the way we prevent ailments, and into the way we identify and treat ailments. Think telehealth: seeing a doctor without "seeing" a doctor. This is another example of the advancements in health, à la technology in the digital world. Remember when we thought WebMD was *the* (online) place to identify an illness without stepping foot into a doctor's office? Telehealth is an example of technology making healthcare more accessible, in other words, democratized. Moving healthcare online enables more people to access healthcare services (by taking geography out of the picture). This is particularly special for accessing specialists in times of urgent need. Often, time is of the essence with health concerns, and telehealth options allow for quicker diagnosis and treatment. Remote-treatment monitoring supports self-care processes and aftercare. Additionally, telehealth technology can be used to see psychiatrists, therapists, and counselors—who help with all things relating to mental health (more on this in the next section).

The digitization of health and healthcare provides X-ray vision into our health and habits. Perhaps the cost of an Apple Watch or an Oura Ring may seem out of budget, but the upside is optimization of health and avoidance of large medical bills in the future. We each have to weigh the pros and cons for ourselves, of course. But it's fair to say that investing in yourself, in your health, is a good move—financially, too.

While technological advancements are advancing visibility into the invisible, thereby informing and changing our lifestyles for the better, there is the potential pitfall of becoming too addicted—dare I say—to technology. Consequently, this is a great segue into discussing mental health.

Mental Health

This particular section (in this chapter) is dedicated to mental health; thereafter, we'll transition to the section on spiritual health. But first, I wanted to point out that the two carry similar archetypal, characteristics, with mental health referring to the health of the mind and spiritual health referring to the health of the spirit.

By definition, and in essence, mental and spiritual health embody the *invisible* archetype, because of their intangible, ethereal nature. What's beautiful is the high value people are placing on the invisible forces of mental and spiritual health. The qualitative aspects of invisible health are hard to pin down, but society is increasingly open to appreciating and prioritizing them anyway. Mental and spiritual health naturally highlight the need to honor *invisible health*. After all, what's the use of having money and a healthy body when your mind is anything but? Your mind and spirit are the operating system of your hardware. Put simply, the mind and spirit animate the physical body.

It's also worth spotlighting that there is a bridge between mental health and physical health. Good mental health positively affects physical health, and good physical health positively affects mental health.[7] This is often referred to as the mind-body connection. Further, adding a temporal element in here, studies show that your mental health in the past affects your physical health at present, and your physical health in the past affects your mental health at present.[8] Our intuition knows this. Because humans have subjectivity, mental health is different for each person—based on each person's complex matrix of being. That said, there are fundamental undercurrents of commonality representing a healthy (and an unhealthy) mind.

In the past, a person's mental state was often discussed in terms of "mental illness" rather than "mental health" or "mental well-being." Mental illness focuses on the presence of disorder, whereas mental health focuses on the absence of disorder. There used to be an emphasis on illness rather than on health, but the sentiment and language shifted around the 1980s, when the topic of mental health became more accessible and better understood.[9] This positive shift in narrative aligns with the current emphasis placed on prevention (rather than treatment), which we also see in the physical health arena. Prevention is now at the forefront of physical and mental health discussions, made possible by all the research and information available on the topic, plus technological advancements within the space.

To preserve a healthy mind, we must consider what causes an unhealthy mind. Ultimately, there are many factors at play, but one thing is for sure: stress is likely involved. Stress is the largest and most prevalent strain on mental health. The tensions of stress comes from many sources, which mirror a lack of each of the *5 Principles of Invisible Wealth*; stress comes from a (perceived) lack of money, health, knowledge, status, influence, time, energy, experiences, and relationships. Our body's stress responses aren't designed to handle the multiple streams of stress that are consistently coming toward us these days, due to our increasingly high-octane, multidimensional world.[10] Because constant stress is so prevalent today, we even have a term for it: chronic stress.

> *"Constant stress draws from the invisible field around our body and depletes our vital life force, leaving little energy for repair and restoration."*
>
> —Dr. Joe Dispenza

Chronic stress impacts both physical and mental health. The American Psychological Association's latest survey revealed that 66% of people said chronic stress causes them physical symptoms, and 63% said chronic stress causes them psychological symptoms.[11] Physically, think diabetes, cancer, and an overall weakened immune system. Psychologically, think anxiety and depression. Studies suggest that American's are more stressed today than they were in the 1990s, largely due to technological shifts creating a nonstop flow of information and expectations from device to person. Additionally, the pressures and stressors of the pandemic certainly boosted this reality. In 2020, at the onset of the pandemic, the focus was squarely on physical health—and rightly so. In 2021, the American Psychological

Association issued a warning of a second pandemic, the pandemic of mental health, that would persist even after the physical threat of the virus was addressed.[12]

We're living in wildly unique times, where external events are beyond the scope of what anyone's seen before. As a result, the effects on our mental well-being are beyond the scope of many people's coping capabilities. We're revisiting our mental models and concept of the world in order to make the day-to-day more manageable. This is inspiring us to think about the way we think. Fortunately, many people can now access psychiatrists, therapists, and counselors through telehealth sessions to help navigate and manage these turbulent waters.

Speaking of water, have you heard of the stress bucket model? It's a model used to visualize and identify what's causing you stress, and what can be done to reduce that stress.[13] It's a constructive analogy and goes something like this: pretend you're holding a bucket, and different streams of stressful events pour into that bucket, gradually filling the bucket up. When you pour water (aka stressful events) into the bucket, it is fine for a time, until the water starts getting too high (aka a breaking point). In order to prevent your bucket from overflowing, you can create holes (stress releases) at the bottom of the bucket to release the water—keeping it from getting too heavy and overflowing. This model helps in conceptualizing the fact that too much stress gets heavy and leads to a mess. Not good. Therefore, managing stress is essential for your mental health.

Uncharacteristically, I'll approach the topic of managing stress with a glass-half-empty perspective, for sake of conversation. Stress is hard to manage, because of its nebulous nature. Stress is the nervous system's response when situations demand more resources than are available; pragmatically, much the same as financial stress. Managing stress is especially challenging when you're unable to peg it to a particular origin, situation, or stream of conflict. However, the holes at the bottom of your stress bucket are designed to release pressure regardless of what stream contributed to the pressure. The more holes, the better; the more stress management tools, the better.

A holistic approach to stress management is essential, so what are the best tools to manage this intangible force? Consider:

1. Physical exercises
2. Breathing exercises

3. Eating nutritious, well-balanced meals
4. Getting proper sleep
5. Limiting alcohol and caffeine intake
6. Connecting with others, laughing
7. Positive thinking
8. Limiting (social) media

These tools are fundamentally familiar, but they too, deserve revisiting. The last tool on the list, limiting (social) media, is an important one, because technology provides a nonstop flow of information and expectations from device to person. While there are positives to this, there are also negatives. Chronic expectations lead to chronic stress, which is why a "media diet" is on the menu of stress management tools. A media diet is to the mind, what a food diet is to the body. The point is to screen your screen time. The phrase "don't let the tail wag the dog" comes to mind. In this context, it means don't let technology control you, but rather, you should control technology. The absence of technology can be just as mentally healthy as the Apple Watch constantly monitoring your physical health—it's all about balance.

We don't know what the future holds, in terms of external stressors and pressures, but we do know that some level of stress will always exist in our lives. It is the inherent nature of this game called life, full of twists and turns. Even positive changes cause stress on our systems, like getting married, receiving a promotion, or having a child. These events are fundamentally positive yet paired with change and, therefore, stress. The key is developing mental strength so that you have the capability and capacity to take things on—head on.

Spiritual Health

Spiritual health, the health of your spirit or soul, is the least definable and quantifiable aspect of health, yet it's receiving lots of attention and priority these days. There are many broad-reaching, fluid definitions of spiritual health—some intertwining with religion, others with the meaning of life. The etymology dictionary provides the following, for "spirit" as a noun:

> Mid 13-c., "animating or vital principle in man and animals," from Anglo-French spirit, Old French espirit "spirit, soul" (12c., Modern French esprit)

and directly from Latin spiritus "a breathing (respiration, and of the wind), breath; breath of a god," hence "inspiration; breath of life," hence "life;" also "disposition, character; high spirit, vigor, courage; pride, arrogance.[14]

Additionally, let's read the definition of spiritual health from the National Library of Medicine for guidance. Its study concluded: "Participants defined spiritual health in three dimensions: religious, individualistic, and material-world-oriented. The study revealed four types of connection in spiritual health: human connection with God himself, with others, and with nature. The majority of participants stated that spiritual health and spirituality were different and pointed out the following characteristics for spiritual health: it affects physical, mental, and social health; it dominates other aspects of health; there are religious and existential approaches to spiritual health; it is perceptible in people's behavior; and it can be enhanced and improved."[15]

To distill this all down, it feels appropriate to say that spiritual health does not relate to the body or the mind, but, rather, something bigger than us, something supernatural that is consequential in the way we find meaning in our lives. It's what we "see" without our eyes and without our minds. That said, it's easy to see why so much value is placed on spiritual health for those it resonates with. The question then becomes, how do we fortify spirit? Timeless tools include:

1. Spending time in nature
2. Expressing gratitude
3. Watching the sunset or sunrise
4. Finding and indulging in your creative outlet
5. Living in the present
6. Practicing yoga
7. Meditating
8. Breathing exercises

Each of these tools embodies the invisible archetype, and you can trust that your intuition knows which tool(s) is best for you. For example, you might turn to the power of positive thought, focusing on the quality of thought. Or to meditation, focusing on the stillness or absence of thought. There are technological innovations that support mental and spiritual health, like meditation and breathwork apps. But ultimately, spending time in nature and watching the sunset is the antitechnology; the antitechnology that updates your software (programming). By definition, or rather, by nature—spirit maintains its integrity by just being, the value of which is not measurable by metrics; it is unquantifiable.

> *"What you think, you become."*
> —*Gautama Buddha*

Beyond technological innovations lays the revisiting of psychedelic therapy to treat and strengthen mental and spiritual health. This therapy includes the use of psychedelic drugs like psilocybin, MDMA, and LSD to treat disorders like depression, anxiety, and post-traumatic stress disorder. "Classic psychedelies like psilocybin and LSD bind to the serotonin receptors, changing how the neurotransmitter experiences mood, cognition, and perception . . . the networks in the brain become more connected and less organized, causing profound changes in consciousness and perception, sense of space, time and reality; the drugs also appear to promote neuroplasticity or the ability of neurons to remodel and form new pathways of communication in the brain."[16] With this in mind, it's understandable why the word *psychedelic* was coined by psychiatrist Humphry Osmond in 1956, meaning "mind-manifesting."[17]

Humans have used psychedelic substances since ancient times, finding psychoactive properties in various plants and fungi. In ancient times, shamans used drugs to access the spiritual world. Fast-forward to the 1950s and 1960s, and much research and use was underway. Peer-reviewed papers, books, and conferences were floating into the minds of many.[18] Psychedelics expanded into consciousness and culture. Take, for example, the fact that Jim Morrison's band (The Doors) took their name from Aldous Huxley's book (*The Doors of Perception*). Huxley's book discusses his experiences with the psychedelic mescaline.[19] Or the Beatles' use of psychedelics as inspiration for much of their music. With expanded use, however, came expanded concern from regulators. In 1970, regulators enacted legislation, classifying many psychedelics as illegal.[20]

Legislation aside, many—including those in the tech world—continued using psychedelics to improve their minds, souls, and . . . work. Famously, Steve Jobs was a proponent of LSD as a tool for unlocking his creative superpowers. That said, perhaps Apple (founded in 1976) was a consequence of psychedelic use; Apple, and other tech innovations that shape our current world (and economy).[21] Today, psychedelic therapy is experiencing a mainstream resurgence, a renaissance, and regulation is looking supportive.

This psychedelic renaissance could have profound implications on the (holistic) health of individuals, and the economy. Here's how: Clinical trials are revealing the mind-bending benefits of psychedelic use, which means economic benefits, as well. The psychedelics market is projected to reach $6.85 billion by 2027, and will likely grow much more as drugs are approved.[22] Needless to say, this is a paradigm shift in the arena of physical, mental, and spiritual health; one that's supportive of health, creativity, connectedness, and innovation.

A final thought. Clearly, people are placing more attention and priority on health—physical, mental, and spiritual health. And with demand comes the opportunity to democratize and monetize. Entrepreneurial minds (perhaps psychedelically inspired) are creating innovative ways to support mindfulness and meditation, through apps like Headspace, Calm, and Breathwrk. These are a few examples of modern technology supporting the use of ancient technology. The wellness market is healthily growing. In a 2021 McKinsey study, it estimated that the wellness market was worth $1.5 trillion, and growing at 5–10% each year.[23] Further, the expectation is a shift toward wellness services (rather than goods)—for example, personal training and counseling. The demand is shifting from the tangible to the intangible, in health, as well.

> *"Whoever values peace of mind and the health of the soul*
> *will live the best of all possible lives."*
>
> —*Marcus Aurelius*

What Is Quality of Life?

The paradigm shifts underway are influencing the way we organize our lives. During the pandemic, many of us revisited and reprioritized what we value (and in most cases, health was top of the list). The most valuable aspects of life are now claiming priority, thereby shape-shifting the infrastructure of our lives. Individuals, and therefore society, are working with values in mind, playing with values in mind, and generally, living . . . with values in mind. Working is how we make money and playing is how we spend money, both of which contribute to the quality of our lives (and the quality of the economy). Additionally, the way we interface with the world is now fundamentally different, because so much has replatformed online: living, working, and playing. So how do we reconceptualize a fulfilled life while these tectonic shifts are in motion?

It starts small: our daily practices are tightly correlated to the quality of our lives. Daily decisions ultimately create the story of your life—one thought at a time, and one decision at a time. Your thoughts, both positive and negative, influence the decisions you make, which is why positive thinking is so important for your mental health and attaining a fulfilled life. The goals you aim for are achieved through the state of your thoughts and decisions. And now more than ever, you can unshackle from the constraints of the past and design for the flexibility of the future. This is a luxury.

Here's a look at quality of life, through the prisms of living, working, and playing.

"Self-sufficiency is the greatest of all wealth."

—*Epicurus*

Living

The quality of your life is built by the quality of your daily decisions. The concept may seem rudimentary, but daily decisions are anything but simple. Nowadays, technological advancements and societal shifts are completely changing what we value and how we organize ourselves. In practical terms, this primarily relates to the way we work and play. Working and playing (socializing) are now available and amplified via technology. We're well aware of the evolving work landscape, considering: remote work, entrepreneurship, the gig economy, creator economy, and the most recent cherry on top, the Great Resignation. Each consideration supports the notion that we are trending toward a landscape where land (geography) doesn't matter.

"Freedom is the greatest fruit of self-sufficiency."

—*Epicurus*

The shift to online has huge implications for quality of life, because it allows us to become geo-flexible or location agnostic. Talent and relationships can live anywhere. We saw a lot of geographical exploration happen as a result of the pandemic, when people started exploring new places to live, even if just for a time. A group of people started to relocate from point A to point B, and others followed. This movement was likely (more significant) because of technology and the influence of social media. People moved like schools of fish, together, in search of an optimal location that supported a higher standard of living (relative to where they came from). People self-organized based on shared values. There was, and remains, a renewed sense of community, more cohesion, support, trust, and therefore well-being. Even if you didn't move geographically, you likely moved sentimentally—closer to those around you, smiling at the woman at your local café, more often than before. Despite all the destruction we collectively experienced, there's an air of romance in the air; the romance for life, falling in love with your life.

Positive daily decisions, whether they relate to physical, mental, or spiritual health, are motivated by the desire to improve your life. And improving your life often leads to improving your health and longevity. With a longer life comes the need for a deeper wallet, to financially sustain and thrive throughout the years. And with a longer life comes the potential for delaying decisions, such as marriage, purchasing a home, and having a child. These decisions contribute to the quality of your life. Financial decisions also contribute to the quality of your life—including how we make and spend our money.

Working

Not to rehash the obvious here, but remote work is a game-changer. Along this same thread, hybrid work is also a game-changer. Think about how much time is saved commuting to and from work. This has huge compounding effects on how we spend our time. The time saved from a 30-minute commute, therefore one hour each day, can be spent on something you value. Your choice. This is a massive win in the realm of enhancing quality of life. And who thought the donut effect (referenced in Chapter 3) sounds anything but healthy?

Quality of life also depends on how often we do what we enjoy. The "how" of working has changed, but so has the "what" along with the "why." Entrepreneurship, the gig economy, and the creator economy are unlocking opportunities to align with work you find enjoyable, interesting, and important. Finding meaning in work plays a huge role in physical, mental, and spiritual health. We're seeing that the pathway to wealth creation can be paved with purpose, and play.

Playing

Play is an important contributor to the quality of life. Yes, play. The *Online Etymology Dictionary* says *play* as a verb is:

> Middle English pleien, from Old English plegan, plegian "move lightly and quickly, occupy or busy oneself, amuse oneself; engage in active exercise; frolic; engage in children's play; make sport of, mock; perform music."[24]

Coincidentally, each descriptor for the etymology of "play" fold into the toolkit for fortifying and improving physical, mental, and spiritual health—all of which are important for quality of life. We came into this world playing as kids. Our default state is to create, to build sandcastles, only to knock them down, knowing we can rebuild the sandcastle again. There's inherent joy in creation, and this joy should be preserved throughout the totality of our lives—whether it finds itself in work or outside of work.

Play, by its essence, is unshackled from the constraints of real boundaries. From a professional perspective, it allows for imagination and human ingenuity—the stuff innovation is made of. From a personal perspective, play lets us connect with others in ways that defy the mundane, constrained elements of life. Play increases positive emotions, bonding, communication, and overall relationship satisfaction, which adds so much to the quality of our lives. This is true of playing online or in real life (IRL). To this end, the gaming industry is booming because the demand for play is booming.

People are reconceptualizing the structures and boundaries of the past, creatively reimaging the future—gamifying life. Gamifying life means treating your life as if it were a game: setting goals, developing a plan, reaching goals, and rewarding yourself. There are even apps available to support in the gamification of life! And with demand comes the opportunity to democratize and monetize. That said, the gaming industry knows no boundaries—no longer constrained by place, time, or physical reality.[25] In a recent Ernst & Young report, it estimated that the gaming industry exceeded $193 billion in global revenue, and the expectation is this growth will continue. By 2025, the gaming industry is expected to generate $211 billion in revenue, with mobile gaming contributing $116 billion.[26] This is yet another example of new marketplaces coming online.

> *"We don't stop playing because we grow old; we grow old because we stop playing."*
> —*George Bernard Shaw*

Chapter 7
The Wealth of Knowledge, Status, and Influence

With a healthy foundation in place, we're ready for the third *Principle of Invisible Wealth*: knowledge, status, and influence. Each of these intangible assets can have profound effects on self, and others, when paired with good intention and use. These assets elevate us, and those around us, to the next level—evolving into the next iteration of self. Oftentimes we forget how powerful it is to share our knowledge, to utilize our status, and to wield our influence for good—benefitting our souls, and benefitting society.

To set the stage, we'll look at the relationship between knowledge, status, influence, and wealth. Thereafter, we'll do a deep dive into each, ultimately arriving at the present-day value of all.

"Share your knowledge. It is a way to achieve immortality."
—*Dalai Lama*

The Relationship Between Knowledge, Status, Influence, and Wealth

Knowledge, specifically the accumulation and use of knowledge, has a powerful relationship with financial wealth, status, and influence. This we intuitively know. But the topic deserves revisiting given the technological advancements and societal shifts underway. Knowledge is a resource for accumulating wealth, and wealth and status are interlinked, because you can pay your way into status and you can monetize status. Plus, as Jordan Peterson points out, "wealth is a proxy for status." Further, influence is often a byproduct of knowledge and status. Fundamentally speaking, it all starts with knowledge.

What *Isn't* Knowledge?

Information Versus Knowledge

From a definitional standpoint, sometimes it's best to know what something isn't in order to know what it is. That said, let's consider the distinction between information and knowledge to better understand what constitutes knowledge.

Every day we are inundated with information, coming to us from smartphones, laptop computers, TV's, and people. Regardless of the medium, information comes to us as data or through observation. Our brains continuously sift through and filter what is useful and relevant, disregarding what is not. Knowledge then occurs as a result of combining information, experience, and intuition.[1] We live our entire lives acquiring knowledge; what we do with it is up to us. Additionally, wisdom is the ability to discern when and how to use your knowledge; in other words, wisdom is the ultimate incarnation of knowledge.

> *"It is the greatest truth of our age: Information is not knowledge."*
> —*Caleb Carr*

We see two familiar themes here we've previously discussed. First, the internet democratized access to information, and technological advancements brought this information into the palms of our hands. An obvious, yet necessary, observation is that we take in troves of information compared to what we consumed in the pre-internet era. Second, our brains are responsible for sifting through all this information, sorting what is and isn't useful, which is where our mental models and thinking patterns come into play. This is why (mental) health is so important, because it determines the filters and models through which we see (and process) the information of the world. Each individual's filters and personal philosophies—human subjectivity—determine the meaning and value of specific information. Our logical brain and emotional brain help us in deciding which information is useful and valuable. For example, I find 0% value in knowing how a toothbrush is made, because the information has no utility to me. Plus, I'm not interested in learning more, out of curiosity, because it's not worth my time or energy.

There's no doubt that the internet democratized access to information. By extension, the democratization of information supports the democratization of knowledge, because you can (more easily) find information that is valuable to you. With this information in mind, let's explore the value of knowledge, status, and influence in today's world.

What Is Knowledge?

I hope that by the end of this section, you'll have new information about the value of knowledge, making you more knowledgeable. Here's a question: What is the importance and purpose of knowledge? The answer is two-pronged:

1. Knowledge is necessary for economic prosperity (surviving).
2. Knowledge is necessary for personal growth (thriving).

Knowing that knowledge is important to surviving and thriving makes it a pretty compelling principle. Knowing, however, is one thing; acting is another. Acquiring knowledge is important but even more so is applying it to benefit your quality of life.

"The purpose of knowledge is action, not knowledge."

—Aristotle

People often have professional goals and personal goals. Maybe it's finding a new job, with higher pay, so you can increase the money you save and invest (P1). Maybe it's meditating 10 minutes a day, to improve your health and quality of life (P2). These goals provide a filtering system for what information is useful (at a point in time of your life). We are constantly sifting through information, acquiring knowledge, and acting on that knowledge to progress our goals. We aim our actions toward our goals, and knowledge informs these actions, which impact our lives.

Using Knowledge

Let's home this knowledge to the hypothetical goal of finding a new job, with higher pay. Assume you are a tax attorney, with 15 years of experience. For the past 5 years, as a hobby, you learned about Bitcoin because you are incredibly interested in the evolving space. Plus, you started getting questions from your clients about how Bitcoin is taxed. Not many, but some. You've listened to and read hundreds of hours' worth of information on Bitcoin, thanks to YouTube and Substack. Over the years, the collective interest in Bitcoin has increased, which means more people are buying it. As a result, this means more people need tax advice for their Bitcoin holdings. As luck would have it, you are knowledgeable in both tax law and now Bitcoin. Given your enhanced knowledge coupled with the high demand for tax attorneys specializing in Bitcoin, you are now well-positioned to find yourself a higher-paying job. Bravo.

> *"You get rewarded for unique knowledge, not for effort. Effort is required to create unique knowledge."*
>
> —*Naval Ravikant*

As you'll recall from Chapter 1, there are three primary considerations when choosing a profession: your interests, your skills, and what the market will reward you for. How you wield your productivity superpowers is unique to you. You discovered that your interest and knowledge in Bitcoin, coupled with your skills and knowledge as an attorney, are something that the market will reward you for, and handsomely. This is an example of specialization, which supports economic prosperity. The father of economics, Adam

Smith, showed us that specialization is healthy for the economy, because it offers increased efficiency and productivity—to you, to your clients, and ultimately to society. This is a net benefit all around.

This hypothetical highlights that increased knowledge has the potential to lead to increased specialization. It also shows that the advancements in technology (in this case, blockchain technology and Bitcoin) have the potential to lead to new marketplaces of work.

The Knowledge Doubling Curve

Knowledge is growing at exponential rates, and the velocity of technological advancements is increasing. This has, and will continue to have, wild implications for the way we make, spend, save, and invest money. Richard Buckminster Fuller, an American inventor and futurist, created the concept of the "Knowledge Doubling Curve" in 1982, after he noticed that until the year 1900, human knowledge doubled approximately every century. By the end of World War II, knowledge was doubling every 25 years. Further, he predicted that our knowledge would double every 12 months by 2020.[2] We are now past 2020, which invites the question: what does the knowledge doubling curve look like today? According to IBM, the build-out of the internet is leading to the doubling of knowledge every 12 hours (industry dependent).[3] Hang on to your seats, friends.

One interesting consequence of the knowledge doubling curve, is the fact that relevant knowledge is increasing faster than we can even absorb. Counterbalancing this, however, is the fact that the useful lifespan of knowledge is decreasing. Becoming comfortable with continuously processing new information and reiterating information, is a must.[4] In our current information paradigm, knowledge really does occur as a result of combining information, experience, and intuition.[5] This is where the elements of creativity and innovation come to the forefront, as we're required to collect and connect dots in ways that look different from the past. The future is creative.

Creative innovation happens by taking new information and melding it with existing information, in novel ways. New and additional information become available, enabling further iterations on the original innovation.

A constant feedback loop is in motion, because of how much and how fast information is coming our way.

Now consider this: the knowledge of money and investment also has exponential power—exponential, wealth-creation power. The more informed you are about making, saving, and investing money, the better equipped you are to use that knowledge for wealth creation purposes. As we saw in Chapter 5, 10 million Americans opened up a new brokerage account in 2020, and access to information had something to do with that.[6] People are increasingly empowered by access to vast knowledge, unlocking monetary upside and human potential. This is just one reason why the *new wealth paradigm* is so promising.

The Knowledge Economy

With all this talk about knowledge and the economy, it only makes sense to layer in the advancements of the knowledge economy. The term *knowledge economy* was first coined by Peter Drucker in his 1969 book, *The Age of Discontinuity*,[7] although it wasn't until the end of the 1990s that the knowledge economy really blossomed.[8] This causes us to ask: What is a knowledge economy? "The knowledge economy is the creation of value using human intelligence. It is considered a fundamental economic shift that is currently underway—based on the observation that a large number of jobs shifted to professions that require extensive knowledge and the ability to create new knowledge."[9]

> *"The future of work consists of learning a living."*
> —*Marshall McLuhan*

The intangible knowledge economy evolved from the tangible industrial economy. "The industrial economy replaced the agrar-ian economy when people left farms for factories; then the knowledge economy pulled them from factories to office buildings. When that happened, the way workers added value changed, too. Instead of leveraging their brawn, companies capitalized on their brains. No longer hired hands, they were hired heads."[10] This shift was, and remains, a result of changes in technology, society, and values.[11] The continued growth and evolution of this economy is based on the accessibility to information and the application of knowledge. Because access to information continues to increase, it stands to reason that the knowledge economy will continue to increase and evolve. People are processing and pivoting faster than before to stay economically relevant. This requires a sense of openness, creativity, and curiosity.

> *"The future belongs to those who learn more skills and combine them in creative ways."*
> —Robert Greene

Needless to say, human capital is a super-asset in the twenty-first century. Regardless of whether you work at a large corporation or for yourself, your intellectual capabilities and contributions carry the potential for economic value creation. Human capital is an asset not listed on a balance sheet, yet drastically impacts the bottom line. We saw this point made during our discussion on the Great Restructuring, which addressed the importance of human capital in implementing and sustaining the restructuring of a business.

What Is Status?

As the saying goes "everything is relative," and status is no exception. A person's status is relative to their society, community, and peers. Therefore, status is a social construct and for that reason, it is often referred to as *social* status. Further, status is innately hierarchical because it holds one individual as more "valuable" over another. This sounds horrible, but it had particular utility during the times of our hunter and gatherer ancestors. Here is a thought experiment: Would you value someone more if you knew they were an excellent hunter and able to bring food back to the village, versus someone who could not? Survival had us befriending the successful hunter, who earned higher status in the village because of the value they could deliver. And others in our village were doing the same; there was a shared belief that mister successful hunter was valuable to the community. Fast-forward a few hundred years, and we still find ourselves valuing some people more than others, granting them higher status within society—albeit, based on different markers. Status is attained through abilities, achievements, associations, and affiliations.

Status Through Abilities and Achievements

In the hunter example, status resulted from his abilities and achievements through hunting. In today's world, status may result from your abilities or achievements through education or occupation—in other words, your ability to gain knowledge, and use knowledge to create value through your work efforts. More often than not, high-status education opens doors to high-status jobs—often, but not always.

In the realm of education, Ivy League schools tend to garner high social status. Ivy League schools garner high social status because they are incredibly selective, historically elite, and academically rigorous. Those deemed capable of excelling in this educational environment are also, by extension, deemed capable of excelling in a professional environment, thereafter. Learn more, earn more. These earnings through income are received in exchange for the value contributed to society. There is a shared belief around this thinking, which in turn, preserves the status quo. Although, this belief is being revisited, as education is being reimagined and redefined.

In the realm of occupation, professions like lawyers and doctors hold high social status. These professions acquire high status, because they require rigorous academic commitment, and contribute vital value to society in the form of saving lives and maintaining social order. These occupations are absolutely necessary for the health and stability of society. That said, their status is utterly warranted. Additionally, other professions are being added to this high-status stratosphere as our society's needs expand and evolve.

The road from high-status education to a high-status job is generally a freeway, but this roadmap is being completely remapped, offering new routes to social status. Entrepreneurs are a great example of those inclined to take the road less traveled. As we saw in Chapter 3, the entrepreneurial spirit animals are alive and well, driving innovation and wealth creation for self and others. Entrepreneurs navigate unchartered territory, reimagining the road to success.

Additionally, small business owners (most of whom don't attend Ivy League schools) create value for society, and do so for the long-term. Notably, small businesses with 500 employees or less, make up 99.9% of all firms in the United States. From 1995 to 2020, these businesses created 12.7 million net new jobs for our economy![12] These small businesses may include medical or legal businesses, but the point is there are many ways to create value for society, which lead to social status.

Entrepreneurs add remarkable value to society through their ambitious endeavors—exploring the path less traveled. Take, for example, Sir Richard Branson, founder of Virgin Atlantic. Branson didn't go to college, but he did start many successful businesses that contribute value across society and across industries: travel, telecommunications, music, and leisure. I had the pleasure of meeting Branson on his island, Necker Island, in the winter of 2019—ahead of the world closing down. His authenticity, magnetism, and kindness were awe-inspiring. You really get the sense that he operates from a place of intuition, from his authentic core. He follows his own roadmap, fueled by vision, executed with drive.

Sir Richard Branson is a prime example for our analysis on status, because he achieved status not only by his professional abilities and achievements, but also by his associations and affiliations. The "Sir" in front of Richard Branson's name is a title bestowed on a man who is recognized for his extraordinary work by the British monarchy. When a man is knighted, he is allowed to use Sir in his title. Being knighted means belonging to the knighthood. This knight, Sir Richard Branson, perfectly illustrates how status can be attained through different pathways. This perfectly transitions us to the next section.

> *"There is no greater thing you can do with your life and your work than follow your passions—in a way that serves the world and you."*
> —*Sir Richard Branson*

Status Through Associations and Affiliations

Status is also earned or granted through association and affiliation. Education and occupation aside, consider the associations or affiliations (perhaps through membership) that are deemed valuable in your society, community, or among your peers. This could be anything from associating with a certain group of friends, to belonging to the local country club (to use a cliché example). Membership to a country club is one instance of how financial wealth and status are interconnected, because you can pay your way into the local country club (i.e., status). Furthermore, it's possible to monetize this status by hosting clients at the golf club and doing business on the turf. Other country club members may be more inclined to do business with you, because you both belong to the same club. Or non-country club members may want to do business with you, because you belong to the country club. Ultimately, status supports making money and financial wealth creation.

The country club membership is a common and familiar example of status granted through association or affiliation, but the membership archetype is changing. Looking across the pond, London is known for its elite members clubs, like Annabel's, 5 Hertford Street, the Arts Club, and newcomers like Maison Estelle. Now, the proliferation of membership clubs is meaningfully moving into cities within the United States. The *Wall Street Journal* published an article in August 2022 titled "Welcome to the Golden Age of the Private Club."[13] Does this mean Americans are becoming more status-oriented? Maybe, maybe not. The general narrative behind this blossoming Golden Age is that the pandemic ushered in the demand for curated spaces, with curated people. This was a catalyst, but what's fueling the sustained growth of membership clubs is that people are valuing intangibles over the tangibles: shared values, a sense of belonging, and curated communities. Plus, there's sharp demand for shared experiences.

Membership clubs are an example of how you can pay your way into status, and many people are lining up for the opportunity, with wallets open. When this *Wall Street Journal* article went to print (August 2022), there were 7,000 people on the waiting list to get into ZZ's, a Miami restaurant and membership club.[14] Further, Soho House had a waitlist of 79,000 people, which is a record number for the company. Soho House first opened in New York City, in 2003; now, there are 38 locations globally.[15] Plus, we're seeing membership clubs, reconceptualized and reimagined, being used for remote workspaces: Chief, NeueHouse, and Zero Bond. People are passing on clothing drenched in logos, and opting to see and be seen in communities that align with their values, interests, and taste.

Although, chasing status through association or affiliation is a slippery slope, because there's no finish line. For this reason, consciously playing the status game is a self-destructive pursuit. I remember one friend telling me that he became addicted to the pursuit of status, caving to the pressure of staying relevant and admired on the global stage. His longtime girlfriend, who is an amazing person, left the relationship because all his time and energy was devoted to accessing the next best thing, the next exclusive event. He has all the social status one could dream of, all the while living in an empty home, albeit with some magnificent art pieces. He has the knowledge, status, influence, and money, yet attained all at the expense of love.

Moving from the physical world to the digital world, let's consider social status on social media. Status on social media platforms is reflected by how many followers you have, how many people engage with your content, and of course, the content itself. Again, it's all relative, but this relativity is morphing when you consider how we now have exposure to more people than those just within our immediate neighborhoods. Whether your associations and affiliations are offline or online, they influence how you are perceived in society. People can infer how you may act in a situation, based upon your associations and affiliations. This inferred information is valuable to society.

Status Symbols

While status isn't (tangibly) visible to the naked eye, status symbols certainly are. The term *status symbol* was coined by German sociologist, Max Weber, to describe the relationship between the goods people buy in connection to their social status.[16] Typically, the good is intended to signify the owner's social standing in society. Status symbols vary between societies, and evolve with time. In antiquity, the Greeks and Romans considered royal purple pigment a status symbol.[17] Today, status symbols include owning a Tesla (tangible) or having a blue check on Twitter (intangible). Status may also be showcased by who or where you vacation, or what member's club you belong to, which can all be shared via social media. Instagram and TikTok, for example, enable the broadcasting of experiences with friends, all the while broadcasting social status. Status symbols are trending from conspicuous consumption to inconspicuous consumption. These two socioeconomic status terms are worth exploring, if interested. Summed up: inconspicuous consumption is "quiet money."

What's also fascinating, tethering the conversation back to Chapter 2, is the move toward values-oriented status. Like values-based spending or conscious consumption, people are touting their associations and affiliations with values-based brands. Basically, luxury goods are out and luxury (values-oriented) lifestyles are in.

> *"Don't worry about the level of individual prominence you have achieved; worry about the individuals you have helped become better people."*
> —*Clayton M. Christensen*

What Is Influence?

The value of influence is inherent in its definition. The definition reveals the utility of influence: the ability or power to affect another person's behaviors or beliefs.[18] Said differently, influence is the ability to inspire, to sway, to motivate others, either in a tangible or intangible way. This is valuable and tremendously important to society. Ultimately, the intention of influence should directly relate to motivating positive change in others, for the benefit of the individual, and society.

Before the internet, all influence was local. People considered the knowledge and social status of others in the community, in determining whether a person held influence in society. People were considered influential if the knowledge they shared had an affect over the behaviors or beliefs of others. Additionally, people were considered influential if their social status had an impact over the behaviors or beliefs of others. For example, a teacher has influence over their student because the knowledge they share has an impact on the student's behaviors or beliefs. I'm sure we all remember one teacher who really influenced us by sparking our curiosities and encouraging life goals. People can influence or be influenced in different ecosystems: in their homes, in their communities, and at their work. This remains the case, although the internet is amplifying the reach and gravity of influence.

> *"Nothing is so potent as the silent influence of a good example."*
> —*James Kent*

Personal Brand and Influence

Here we are again, with another example of how the internet changed the value dynamics of a fundamentally familiar concept—in this case, influence.

The internet enables people to "scale" their influence in local communities, in the wider world, and in the digital world. With this grand optionality at hand, people are considering how their identity translates online. Intentionality definitely goes into architecting an online identity, or as we now call it—a personal brand. The term *personal branding* was coined by Tom Peters in his 1997 article titled "The Brand Called You."[19] In his article, Peters addresses the relationship between personal brand and influence. A personal brand is used to grow influence. And influence is used to motivate others and monetize for yourself. Therefore, it's important to ask the question of what change do you want to motivate in others? What value do you want to deliver to the world? These questions roll out the red carpet and invite us to analyze ourselves, and how we interface and present to the world.

Branding was traditionally reserved for corporations, but now people are branding themselves just like corporations always have. We're living in a time where "the company" takes on an archetype of an individual and "the individual" takes on the archetype of the company. Companies recognize that a relatable brand personality is key for business success—particularly these days (a nod to the Great Restructuring currently underway). We form opinions about companies, just as we do about people. That said, consumers want to connect and know what values a company represents—what the company stands for. A company might exhibit or embody the same attributes as a friend or a trusted ally. The through line here, the theme we keep seeing, is that people (both investors and consumers) are placing a high premium on values: values-based investing, values-based spending, values-based companies, and values-based brands.

On the flip side, individuals are taking on the archetype of the company. This reminds me of the Jay-Z lyric: "I'm not a businessman, I'm a business, man." Individuals are considering the value and influence they can offer—and how to do so, both online and offline. People are exploring their relevance in the marketplace, and clearly articulating their value proposition. Personal branding, I believe, isn't about portraying something that isn't there (inauthentic), but, rather, showing what *is* (authentic). For so long, many corporate cultures required conformity—in both appearance and ideals. But over time, cultural shifts are celebrating authenticity—in all its forms—untethered from the narrowly defined conformity of the past.

Our ability to distinguish and differentiate is now admired. In fact, it's required from a personal brand and influence perspective. This is great for business, because consumers love authenticity. Sex sells, but so does authenticity. This really puts a new perspective on the saying: "Take care of yourself, you are your most valuable asset" by Matshona Dhliwayo.

The internet, social media platforms specifically, astronomically amplify the reach and richness of knowledge, status, and influence. The question then becomes: What are you amplifying? What beliefs and behaviors are you motivating in others? There's a social responsibility inherent in the ability to wield influence. We must strive to put forth a model (meaningful) life, versus a model (superficial) life, by modeling the value of values.

The Influencer Economy

Speaking of models, some people associate "influencers" with models posing in swimsuits on Instagram—although the influencer economy is anything but just models in swimsuits. The term *influencer* within the context of the influencer economy refers to those having a large following and impact on the beliefs and behaviors of their followers. Influencers make money in several ways, one of which is being hired as an ambassador for a corporate brand. What does this mean? It means a company hires an influencer to represent the brand to increase brand awareness. Companies turn to influencers they feel represent the brand personality, and influencers engage with companies who are aligned with their personal brand. It's a reciprocal partnership that is authentic. Simply put, these partnerships work best when there is an alignment of values. Influencers help market a company's product to a new audience, *their* audience. As long as the influencer's endorsement is positive and authentic, then their followers may consider buying the company's product. The intention is for the influencer's influence to sway purchasing decisions in favor of the company's product.

Corporations traditionally turn to A-list celebrities as brand ambassadors, but they are now turning to influencers, too—particularly as a conduit to millennial and Gen Z consumers.[20] This makes sense, when you consider the hyper-personalization and conscious consumption that these two generations are demanding. In my mind, influencers, archetypally, sit at the intersection between a celebrity and a friend. Some consumers find influencers more relatable and, therefore, feel a closer connection to the endorsement—assuming the endorsement is authentic. Data from September 2019, compliments of Morning Consult, show that about half of millennials and Gen Z consumers trust influencer recommendations when deciding whether to make a purchase.[21]

Serendipitous anecdote: Morning Consult provides brand intelligence analytics (among other data). Coincidentally, I watched Morning Consult's co-founder, Kyle Dropp, build his personal brand all the while building the company, which is currently valued at over $1 billion.[22] He's a prime example of someone who masterfully wove knowledge, status, and influence together, and did so—authentically. Kyle carries all the hallmarks of these intangible assets. First, he has academic achievements at Stanford and Princeton. Second, his previous occupation was as a professor at Dartmouth. Third, his status is fortified through all the associations he's affiliated with. But what's most important is the inspiration he ignites within those around him—his influence.

Kyle used to host dinners at his New York City apartment, curating a group of interesting people to share a meal together. During each dinner, he presented a question to the group, and everyone shared their answers. I vividly remember one question: *What are your three favorite brands?* I answered Harpers Bizarre, Doc Martens, and Four Seasons Hotels. Kyle created so much value for his dinner guests by making sure each person had the opportunity to introduce themselves and to share what they were working on. He also proactively introduced people with common interests and goals—a master connector. And he did so without asking for anything in return. To me, this is the epitome of influence—utilizing the asset for the greater good.

Perhaps you know the book *How to Win Friends and Influence People* by Dale Carnegie. This book, originally published in 1936, sold over 30 million copies worldwide, making it one of the best-selling books of all time.[23] In his book, Carnegie lists timeless principles for winning friends and influencing people. This book predates the internet and influencer economy, but it goes to show that people have always placed great value on influence.

Whether your intention is to monetize influence or not, there is no denying that influence is valuable and its utility is derived from your knowledge, your status, and your personal brand. By the end of 2022, the influencer economy is expected to reach $16.4 billion.[24] For perspective on how fast this market is growing, it was valued at a mere $1.7 billion in 2016.[25] This industry stands on the shoulders of platforms such as Instagram, TikTok, Facebook, and YouTube. These technological innovations are expanding networks, and increasing the utility of information—birthing new economies, thereby providing additional avenues for wealth creation.

Having a wealth of knowledge, status, and influence is power, especially when translated into monetary gain. People are considered powerful when they have an abundance of one or all of these attributes. The way to attain outward power is by mastering your internal power, or personal power. The accumulation of knowledge, status, and influence all require an element of self-knowing and self-mastery, which is invisible to the outside world. While your internal power ultimately reveals itself to the outside world, there's less emphasis on parading it around in today's culture. The theatrics around power parading are dissolving; humility and authenticity are raining all over the power parades. The current paradigm shift supports the influencing and advancing of society forward, in stealth mode.

"The measure of a man is what he does with his power."

—*Plato*

Chapter 8
The Wealth of Time, Energy, and Experiences

W e now know the value of gaining knowledge, status, and influence (P3), which each require time, energy, and experience. For example, knowledge is the result of blending information, experiences, and intuition together, and it takes time to acquire. Status is the result of persevering, to excel and achieve. Furthermore, to be truly influential, you must possess the necessary knowledge and status to share with others, enabling your influence to emanate from an informed and powerful position. This provides a great segue and preview into the fourth *Principle of Invisible Wealth* (P4).

> *"A man who dares to waste an hour of time has not discovered the value of life."*
>
> —*Charles Dickens*

The Relationship Between Time, Energy, Experiences, and Wealth

Time has a powerful relationship with energy, experiences, and financial wealth. Given the increased demands on our time these days, we're becoming more conscientious of how we "spend" it. We intuitively know that how we spend our time impacts all other resources. But how we allocate our time looks fundamentally different from times past, because of technological advancements and societal shifts. Technological innovations offer the potential to drain or improve our happiness. Further, time and energy are inextricably interconnected, because how you spend your days depends on the amount of vitality you have. In reverse, the amount of vitality you have depends on how you spend your days. Additionally, time and energy provide the potentiality for, and influence the quality of, experiences. Ultimately, the goal is to turn time and energy into money, which can then be used to optimize time and energy—fully experiencing life.

"Wealth is the ability to fully experience life."
—*Henry David Thoreau*

What Is Time?

Time, many would say, is the most important asset we have. I agree. Let's take the time to talk about time. Time is defined and described as the continual sequence of events that occurs, in irreversible succession. These events move from the past, through the present, and into the future. Additionally, time is a quantity measurement used to sequence events.[1] This sequencing helps us to structure our lives. As Albert Einstein said, "time is what clocks measure." Clocks are based on seconds, minutes, and hours. Calendars are based on days, months, and years. Both help us to organize ourselves within the world.

It's interesting to think about time, from a definitional perspective, because it's an asset we're each born with and know so intimately. Yet, while we each know how many hours are in a day, we don't know how many days we'll get; we never know how much future is remaining. Life is ephemeral and fragile, which is my primary reason for writing this book. I felt an intuitive ping to use my time, energy, and experiences to develop the concept and framework of *Invisible Wealth*.

> *"You could leave life right now. Let that determine what you do and say and think."*
>
> —*Marcus Aurelius*

In April 2022, I left my job to fully commit myself to *Invisible Wealth*. This makes me part of the Great Resignation statistics. I traded my stable, lucrative job for the unknown—a financial opportunity cost. But what I did know was that I would have full authority over how I organize my days and where I place my attention. It also gave me full authority over where I was geographically. At a point in my life, this is what I valued the most. It was possible to take this financial risk because I worked really hard to save and invest my money. Sitting on top of a comfortable cash cushion mitigated the uncertainty of taking this risk—a risk I hope contributes positively to society, to the *new wealth paradigm* emerging.

I worked hard to save and invest my money for many reasons, but, candidly, I never imagined leaving my job would be one of them—until the world and my personal philosophy dramatically shifted. My financial goals were always simple: save and invest as much money as possible. I grew up in a thrifty home. There was a time when my mom and I lived in a furnished basement, and ate rice and beans for dinner, regularly. Basements can be particularly cold, especially during the winter months in Canada. Instead of turning up the heat, mom would suggest I put on a sweater. Electricity for heating cost money; putting on a sweater did not. Year-round, mom only bought what we needed. Needless to say, simplicity and minimalism is in my DNA.

As it turns out, this minimalistic approach to life is very on brand these days. We shift away from consuming tangibles, and to consuming intangibles—experiences included. Having less things on hand leads to less maintenance and less distraction, which is important when we consider the time value of money and the monetary value of time. Money saved and invested versus spent on an additional set of x, y, and z, is a smart move for both your time and your money.

Time Value of Money

I was always in the mentality of save today, for the benefit of tomorrow; foregoing the unnecessaries—it was this or that, not this and that. Life is full of trade-offs, particularly when it comes to time—and money. There's a concept called the *time value of money*, which means the value of money today is worth more than that same amount of money tomorrow (aka in the future).[2] Logically, if you receive $100 today, then you can immediately use or invest it today. Either way, the $100 today has utility. However, if you receive $100 one year from now, the money doesn't have utility until then (all things being equal). So, everyone wants money and they want it now. This is the financial principle of the time value of money and is also referred to as time-preference of money. We saw this financial principle in action in Chapter 5, when looking at the power of investing over a 21-year period. If you invested $100,000 into the public equity market, which returned about 6.9% from 2000 to 2021, then your $100,00 would be $406,005 by 2021. This is the power of time, money invested, and our good friend, compounding.

Monetary Value of Time

While saving and strategizing, leading up to my very own Great Resignation, I began calling into question what many of us often think about: What is my time really worth? This is called the monetary value of time. There are different ways to calculate the value of your time in dollar terms. Here's an example using the most straightforward, approach.[3] Let's say you make $100,000 a year as an accountant. Then let's assume your typical work week is Monday through Friday, 9 a.m. to 5 p.m. (40 hours per week × 52 weeks in the year). That places you working 2,080 hours per year. Finally, we take the total money you earn in a year divided by the total time spent earning that money in a year, and voila, your time is worth $48 per hour. This easy calculation adds valuable perspective to how much time and energy we give things in our lives. Stressing over the traffic jam this morning? Not worth your time. And as your earning potential increases, so does the monetary value of your time. Usually, your earning potential increases with time, energy, and increased experience.

That said, as the years roll forward, your earning potential increases while your time remaining decreases. This is, fundamentally, the reason why we tend to reprioritize later in life, prioritizing the intangibles of life over the tangibles. But for many this reprioritization is happening now, regardless of age.

> *"Trade money for time, not time for money. You're going to run out of time first."*
>
> —*Naval Ravikant*

Knowing the monetary value of your time helps in determining and prioritizing what's most important; it shapes your relationship with time. We begin thinking about investing hours/time, just the same as we think about investing dollars/money.

Taking this one step further, consider the non-monetary value of your time. By this, I mean consider: Where is your time (and energy) going? What are you supporting each hour of the day? in terms of work or otherwise. Are you spending 40 hours a week on meaningful work, propelling society forward in a positive, consequential way? These intangible considerations are important. Imagine earning a whopping $1 million a year, with each work hour worth $500, but you're making this money by doing things that are a net-negative for you or society. This dilutes the value of your working hours, even though it's not monetary dilution. Perhaps the stress of your annual $1 million paycheck is wreaking havoc on your mind, body, and spirit, and taking years off your life. Meaningful work that is a net-positive for you and society increases the value of your hours. Quality use of your time is just as important as the quantity used.

It's worthwhile pulling forward the concept of multiple streams of income and passive income from Chapter 5. First, having multiple streams of income is a smart way to structure your cash flow, so you have multiple incomes coming to you from different sources, at different times. This is particularly important if some streams pay semi-annually, because of the time value of money principle. For example, let's assume one stream of income pays semi-annually, meaning you receive $25,000 every January and $25,000 every June. Your January payment has more value to you because you can spend or invest it earlier in the year. Your June payment does not have value to you until half way into the year, when you can spend or invest it at that time. I'm sure if you had your way, receiving $50,000 in January each year would be preferred, because you could spend and/or invest the money sooner rather than later. As we know, the sooner you invest money in the market, the sooner it has the potential to grow.

Second, passive income allows you to generate income with minimal investment of time and energy. By definition, passive income is earned through little participation and involvement. This directly translates into having more time to do other things, besides working for purposes of generating income. Tim Ferriss talks about this in his book *The 4-Hour Work Week.*

Technology and Time

With a grand premium placed on time, it's understandable why we want to optimize it. Consequently, technological advancements aim at improving our relationship with time. Over the century, technology has improved access to information, communication, transportation, productivity and efficiency. Here's a household example: fridges. In 1913, the refrigerator became available for home use.[4] Fridges extend the shelf-life of food and it's nutrients, which are so vital for our well-being and vitality. Visualize everything in your fridge right now, and consider how refrigeration optimizes time. Perhaps you even order your groceries online with delivery straight to your door. It's astonishing. As time goes on, additional iterations and innovations help us to manage this precious resource. The apps on your phone, most likely, highlight this point. Specifically, Uber spares you from standing on the street corner with your arm in the air, for an unknown length of time. Online banking makes it possible to deposit a check with a few clicks of a button, versus driving a few miles down the road to your local bank. These are time savers. However, it's possible the apps on your phone are stealing your precious time. We're all guilty of overscrolling or checking our phones in anticipation of a ping. The "attention economy" commoditized our time, which is why it's so important to consider where your curiosity goes. As Tony Robbins says, where your energy flows, your attention goes.

The goal is to leverage technology, to optimize time and energy.

What Is Energy?

The concept and definition of energy takes on different interpretations depending on context, but simply, it's the ability to do work.[5] Energy is the vitality required to sustain physical or mental activity, and it comes from the wellsprings within; the physical, mental, and spiritual wellness of a person.[6] Your health is the source of your vitality, which is why making time for health is so incredibly important. The way you spend your time influences the amount of energy you have. And in the reverse, the amount of energy you have influences the way you spend your time. While this appears like a chicken-or-the-egg paradox, I'd venture to say that how you structure and utilize your time informs how much energy you have.

Energy and Work

Modern civilization is possible because society learned to convert energy from one form into another form.[7] People use energy to walk, to drive cars, to cook food, to teach students, and to program code—along with many other tasks.[8] Some of these activities are done in exchange for money, while others are not. You can use your energy to be a cook at a restaurant, to become a teacher at a school, or to program code for a new tech start-up. From an economics perspective, the more efficient you are with your energy, the more productive your output is over time. Simply put, the more efficient the input, the more productive the output. This is where we start to see the relationship between energy, work, and money coalesce. Let's home in on how we convert our energy at work, thereby making money in exchange for our efforts.

Work is called work because it requires the exertion of energy. The type and amount of energy exerted depends on the nature of your work. If you're a construction worker, you're exerting mostly physical energy. If you're a software engineer, you're exerting mostly mental energy. Either way, the quality of your health impacts the amount of energy you have to expend on work, and therefore impacts how much money you can make. In order to preserve energy for other things besides work (living and playing), it's clever to consider working smarter versus working harder.

Managing Time and Energy

In conversation, we hear the saying, "pay attention." This expression implies two important characteristics of attention: it is limited and it is valuable (just like time). When we "pay" attention to one thing, we deplete our budget of mental resources, thereby having less attention available to spend elsewhere."[9]

Managing time and energy is different today, than merely five years ago because of technological advancements and cultural shifts. As a consequence, there are new distractions and new priorities at play. But one thing remains, managing time requires consistent discipline. Let's consider the major pulls on time and energy (attention): technology and stress.

First, it's no surprise that technology saves us lots of time, but it also wastes lots of time, too. In the United States, 46% of Americans believe they spend an average of four to five hours on their phones each day. On the extreme end of the spectrum, 11% claim to spend seven or more hours on their phones each day; that's nearly a day's work. Let's slice the data another way: 67.3% of millennials say they are on their phone more than preferable, of which 30.5% are taking steps to reduce their screen time. Among Gen Z's, 76.3% are on their phones more than preferable, with 41% taking steps to reduce their screen time. According to research, 51.8% of people use social media apps out of boredom. Further, 42.8% of people associate screen time with trouble paying attention.[10] The numbers speak for themselves; technology is a major pull on time and energy (attention).

Second, stress depletes our resources, namely time and energy. As we'll recall from Chapter 6, stress can come from many sources, and continuously, resulting in chronic stress. This tension negatively effects our body, mind, and soul, which compromises the wellspring of our vitality. When our vitality is compromised, so too is our ability to work. Many even say that money is a form of energy.

Stress definitely pulls on time and energy. Life will always bring some level of stress in our lives, some more so than others. But the reasons for our stressors are changing shape and texture. An obvious example: big life changes caused by the pandemic. Everyone reading this has a story and experienced a stressful challenge as a result of the pandemic. Odds are, you're still managing the forced pressures from this historical time. Many feel like nomads, not in body but in mind. Our minds are moving from one thing to the next, which is exactly why managing our time and energy is so important. Being intentional with decisions and actions helps to prevent and alleviate stress. That said, let's look at how to best manage time, which in turn helps in managing energy and attention other resources.

> *"The price of anything is the amount of life you exchange for it."*
> —*Henry David Thoreau*

The secret to managing time and energy (attention) is a combination of intentionality and consistent discipline. Here are ways to work smarter, not harder, using your resources in prudent ways.

1. Single-tasking (versus multi-tasking)
2. Using phone with intentionality, and as leverage
3. Ritualizing sleep time
4. Saying no to things that are not value-adds
5. Healthy, nutritious intake (food and media)
6. Minimalizing/simplifying
7. Using calendar time blocks
8. Turning off notifications on your phone

The Pareto Principle

Your time plus your energy, equals your life. Reason, it's absolutely worth thinking about how to align your time with your energy in productive ways. *Pareto Principle,* otherwise known as the 80/20 rule. This principle states that 80% of consequences come from 20% of causes. Italian economist and sociologist, Vilfredo Pareto, discovered this principle when he observed and researched the distribution of wealth within society. He found that a large portion of wealth was held by a small portion of the population.[11] Many have gone on to apply this principle to other areas of economics and business.

That said, let's apply this principle to time and energy management, highlighting the potential for increasing productivity in work (money) goals. The Pareto Principle supposes that 80% of your results will come from

20% of your efforts. With this in mind, evaluate your tasks, and prioritize the 20% that will provide 80% of what you value. This principle helps in prioritizing and focusing on the activities that have the biggest potential impact on your goals. Further, it's best to use your peak time and energy for the most impactful tasks, those that are often harder than the less impactful tasks, yet stand to yield the highest reward. Deep work often translates into deep and meaningful results, in shorter amounts of time.[12]

> *"Distraction is dilution."*
>
> —*Unknown*

The Attention Economy

Attention is a scarce, intangible asset and one of the most valuable resources in the digital age. Your attention is valuable to you, and it's also valuable to businesses. Businesses are well aware of the potential to convert attention into dollars, which is why so many companies are competing for your time and energy. Companies distribute targeted marketing ads based on the data they constantly mine from your activity online. More attention means more sales, so there's a clear incentive to draw people in and maintain their gaze for as long as possible. American psychologist and economist, Herbert Simon, coined the term "*attention economy*," and made the clever observation that in an information-rich world, a wealth of information results in the poverty of attention.[13]

Advertising plays a huge role in the attention economy. The way ads are distributed and presented is changing rapidly as the battle for attention gets uber competitive. Facebook and Instagram are testing augmented-reality advertisements.[14] Others are making user interface adjustments, making it harder to avert and divert your eyes elsewhere. It's all really bonkers. The attention economy is valued at billions of dollars.[15]

While an intentional social media diet may provide reprieve from the draws on your attention, Web3 might provide a more meaningful counterbalance in the future. Remember how I mentioned that companies are able to do targeted marketing based on all the data constantly being mined from your activity online? Well, Web3 would stave off this data mining by enabling users to own their own data. This means you would control who sees your data and what is done with it.[16] Basically, your gold mine of data would be placed into your hands, rather than into the hands of businesses and advertisers. This is another example of individual empowerment, a theme woven throughout each of the *Principles of Invisible Wealth* thus far.

While this may be a bit down the road, it's notable and promising to see people placing their attention on redefining the power dynamics in the attention economy.

What Are Experiences?

We use our time, energy, and money to experience life fully. The dictionary describes an experience as "something personally encountered, undergone, or lived through" and "the act or process of directly perceiving events or reality."[17] Experiences come in many forms including: educational, professional, travel, and entertainment, for example. These are all in addition to typical, commonplace "life experiences"—the mundane or trite. Some experiences are planned, whereas others, not so much. Some experiences are positive, whereas others, not so much. And as life goes on, so does the multiplicity of these experiences. The bottom line: there are many ways to deconstruct the concept of experience. For purposes of our exploration, let's focus on the fun and familiar stuff—the extraordinary and ordinary.

Extraordinary Experiences

Extraordinary experiences add a rich dimension to life, the value of which is reflected in society and in the economy. We're witnessing the shift from spending on tangibles, i.e., goods, to spending on intangibles, i.e., experiences. In the United States, the top 1% have spent less on material goods since 2017 (and are now spending more on education and healthy lifestyles).[18] We saw this through the lens of status symbols in Chapter 7, when discussing how people are forgoing luxury goods for luxury lifestyles, i.e., memberships and experiences. The 1% aside, millennials are leading the way for prioritizing and purchasing experiences.[19] Among millennials, 78%

are spending their time, energy, and money on experiences over materials.[20] This generation isn't valuing the traditional markers of success, like buying a car, but, rather, on experiences instead. A McKinsey report blends these points together, and also folds in the role social media is playing in the prolific demand for experiences: "The fact that millennials are now the largest spending cohort, and that the cohort of higher-income consumers is growing as well, creates greater confidence in the sustainability of the trend. To understand the underlying drivers of this shift in consumer spending behavior, we see three key factors, which are particularly applicable to millennials but hold true among older consumer cohorts too: a more holistic perspective on what leads to happiness, the growing importance of social media, and an increasing fear of missing out. They are unlikely to dissipate, which suggests that this shift in spending behavior will stick."[21]

Agreeing with the three key factors this McKinsey report lays out, let's explore each, starting with the quest for *happiness*. Happiness can be found through experiences for a few reasons. First, we often share experiences with other people. Sharing experiences with others is a way to form strong social bonds, which we all crave. Humans are social, by nature; we are literally hardwired to connect. It's a necessity, and this necessity became glaringly obvious when we were all quarantining in seclusion for months on end. Human connection through shared experiences makes us happy.

Second, experiences typically provide a great(er) return on investment. The joy we get from purchasing a new object usually declines with time. Joy typically declines anywhere from six to eight weeks and up to three months, after purchase.[22] The happiness of seeing the new shiny object on our table, in our closet, or in our garage—fades with time. Plus, objects require maintenance. And when you have lots of objects, this translates into lots of upkeep and maintenance (aka time and energy). Not only that, but the value of the object may actually fade too—aka depreciate in value (e.g., cars). Experiences and memories stay with us for a lifetime, whereas objects don't.

Third, extraordinary experiences make us feel alive, they stretch us. They allow us to explore the continuum of being. And sharing this aliveness, this stretching into realms unknown, with others— is priceless. After all, the reason for intentionally managing our time, energy, and money is to fully experience life, to feel, to max out our aliveness and our sense of vitality.

We share these experiences with others in the moment, and we can also share the story of the experience with others, thereafter. Take for example, attending a dinner party or a work gathering; what do most people talk about, besides the weather—their experiences. Therefore, there's this sort of compounding effect from the extraordinary experience that lives on beyond its initial occurrence.

> *"The very purpose of life is to experience life in its fullest depth and dimension."*
>
> —*Sadhguru*

Extraordinary experiences make us feel alive because they deviate from the norm, from the mundanity of the day-to-day. Some of us search for "peak experiences," those described by psychologist Abraham Maslow, as profound and meaningful events.[23] These awe-inspiring moments are saturated in feelings of pleasure and bliss. Whether extraordinary or awe-inspiring, the experiences are etched into the essence of our being, and are anything but mundane. However, the mundane, the day-to-day moments provide just as much opportunity to shape our lives as the peak moments do. Let's draw a parallel between peak experiences and peaks in the stock market.

There's a parallel between investing money (energy) into the stock market cycle and investing time and energy throughout life. Often, both as an investor and as an individual, we seek the peaks. In other words, we seek the market highs and peak experiences, yet the market lows and mundane moments deserve equal emphasis. A savvy investor knows how to optimize market dips, just the same as a savvy individual knows how to optimize mundane moments. As an investor looking for investment opportunities, you can view a bad market as a great time to invest. As an individual looking for valuable experiences, you can view the mundane moments as a great time to rest, reflect, and recharge—which are necessary for truly enjoying (peak) experiences with self and others. Additionally, moments of solitude provide the space for self-inquiry, which is incredibly valuable (for reasons we'll explore in the next chapter). Finding opportunity in both the ups and downs allows you to fully appreciate the market cycles and the cycles of life—the totality of being.

> *"Content with an ordinary life, you can show all people the*
> *way back to their own true nature."*
>
> —*Lao Tzu*

Ordinary Experiences

The mundane moments, the trite to-dos, are valuable. Why? Because the extraordinary experiences are measures against the ordinary; the ordinary acts as the benchmark. Beyond this, time, as we know, is precious and finite, and ordinary experiences make up most of our time. If time is precious, then it follows that so too are our daily, ordinary experiences.

> *"The real voyage of discovery consists not in seeking new*
> *landscapes, but in having new eyes."*
>
> —*Marcel Proust*

Now let's address the elephant in the room: What about bad experiences? Wisdom suggests those are precious, too. As we all know, life is full of twists and turns, which sometimes lead to dark places. This is life, they say. But what "they" also say is that wisdom is found in these dark places. These experiences also stretch us, across the continuum of being. And bad experiences can be channeled into valuable lessons. There are times when we color with yellow, with green, with pink pencils, and there are times we color with black, with brown, with gray. All are necessary contributors to a beautifully drawn and colored life.

Challenging experiences invite us to view life in different ways or through different lenses. Pencils are sharpened during these times, under pressure. The precision with which you're left, helps in dealing with the next (bad) experience, with well-informed accuracy. As Will Rogers said, "Good judgment comes from experience, and a lot of that comes from bad judgment." Better yet, some people say that learning from other people's experiences is the best teacher, by hearing or reading about their lives, and lessons—sparing you the scraped knee or broken heart.

Experience Economy

Something of value? There's an economy for that, and the (extraordinary) experience economy is no different. It's projected that the experience economy will reach $12 trillion by 2023.[24] This projection is supported by the fact that we've already seen a massive shift in spending four times more on experiences, versus buying physical goods.[25] This massive shift is in alignment with the other trends we're seeing, namely, the shift away from buying things. Many are less inclined to own cars (as previously mentioned), given the rise of the sharing economy. Many are more inclined to share experiences with others in person, counterbalancing the hours spent online. Essentially, there are a myriad of factors influencing the rise of the experience economy. What's more, technological innovation promises to enhance our experiences; entering from left stage, in comes, the metaverse.

> *"The metaverse is the next level of the 'try before you buy'*
> *concept, and it offers new vectors for advertisers and marketers alike, and*
> *they should not be underestimated, no matter how we*
> *feel about a virtual universe."*
> —Simone Puorto

The metaverse offers experiences beyond our physical world, hence its name. Meta comes from a Greek word meaning "after" or "beyond," and is often used as a prefix meaning "more comprehensive" or "transcending."[26] And that's exactly the intention of the metaverse right now, to go beyond our current universe by offering experiences that immerse and transcend the norm. The metaverse is an umbrella concept that covers terms such as augmented reality, virtual reality, mixed reality, virtual economies, headsets, and digital glasses. It relates to a continuum of immersive experiences, which are value-adds for learning, working, or playing.[27] The metaverse has the potential to extend our experiences; it's a feature, added to certain experiences. As Albert Einstein said, "Life is just like a game . . . ," and the metaverse is here to prove it.

There's clearly a fundamental shift in our concept of value within society and therefore, within the economy. We walked through the various economies pegged to the 5 *Principles of Invisible Wealth*: the creator economy, the knowledge economy, the influencer economy, the attention economy, and the experience economy, to name a handful. The through line: each of these economies are valuing intangible assets; an abundance of which results in *Invisible Wealth*.

Chapter 9

The Wealth
of Relationships
with Self and Others

Human connection makes us happy, so much so that we want to experience the extraordinary and the ordinary with others. In fact, our lives circulate around relationships; relating, not relating, and everything in between. We learn so much about ourselves, and others, through interpersonal relationships. Relationships consistently invite us to revisit, reimagine, and redefine who we are and what we value, by virtue of our interactions with other people, and vice versa. Further, the who and how of interacting in the digital world is progressing connection into new frontiers; relevancy now trumps proximity.

As the saying goes, "What we see in others is a reflection of ourselves." Carl Jung famously shared that everyone is our mirror. Every single person in our life mirrors back to us parts of ourselves, allowing us to see the qualities within that we admire or dislike (by virtue of the relationships with others). Our inner reality reflects in our outer reality, relationships included. A friendly welcome to the fifth, and final, *Principle of Invisible Wealth* (P5).

The Relationship Between Our Relationship with Self, Others, and Wealth

The relationship with self and others is inherently interconnected because our relationship with self serves as the foundation from which all other relationships are built. A baseline relationship with self is always intact, although others help us to fortify or restructure our foundations, when needed. This baseline foundation is the initiation point from which all other relationships are built. As Esther Perel says, "relationships have the potential to shape our lives," so it's preferable that each relationship starts and grows from a point of strength, as with anything else in life; the stronger the foundation, the better the build. Our relationships shape our work, our families, and our enjoyment, which is why they are so fundamentally important to the quality of our lives. Further, our relationships influence our wealth, and our wealth influences our relationships. We'll unpack this throughout the chapter.

What Is a Relationship with Self?

"One secures the gold of the spirit when he finds himself."
—*Claude M. Bristol*

We all desire intimate, meaningful relationships with friends, family, and lovers, but the most intimate relationship you'll ever have is with yourself. The person you'll spend the most time with, talk the most with—is yourself. The question then becomes, what are you saying to yourself?

The Greek maxim "Know thyself" represents the philosophy of self-knowledge or self-knowing. Having an awareness of your beliefs, thoughts, and emotions shines light on the whys behind your decisions and actions—how you orient yourself in the world. This knowledge of self is critically important when you consider that your beliefs, thoughts, emotions, decisions, and actions all impact your wealth of money, investment, health, quality of life, knowledge, status, influence, time, energy, experiences and relationships with yourself and others. Therefore, any investment into knowing yourself better, is an unequivocal win. Progress toward physical (body), mental (mind), and emotional (heart) mastery is the key to unlocking your fuller potential.

This sounds great, but when and how do you cultivate self-knowing? This awareness develops from both extraordinary and ordinary experiences (with yourself and others). For a start, extraordinary experiences stretch, awaken, and inspire you by revealing aspects of yourself that may otherwise remain dormant. This expands self-knowing, into terrain otherwise unexplored. Ordinary experiences reflect your patterns, your standard way of being, which is also illuminating. All experiences and interactions with others provide insight into yourself, which is why engaging, listening, and learning from people is so valuable. Interpersonal relationships are vehicles for personal growth. It's great to be with others to share experiences and thoughts, although this should be balanced out by spending time alone. Moments of solitude allow time to reflect on these experiences and interactions. There's great value in spending time alone, providing yourself with the space to reflect, reexplore, refine, and even redefine aspects of self.

> *"He who knows others is clever; He who knows himself has discernment."*
> —*Lao Tsu*

Spending time in a bubble bath while holding a glass of champagne might embody self-love and reflection, but there are more ways than one. In 2015, The *New York Times* published an article titled "The 36 Questions That Lead to Love."[1] This article is based on research by psychologist Arthur Aron, who presented a practical methodology for creating interpersonal closeness in his study.[2] The *New York Times* article lays out 36 questions to ask someone, in order to foster interpersonal closeness and intimacy. These 36 questions are divvied up into three sets, with the first 12 questions being the least probing and the last 12 questions being the most probing. These questions are intended to unveil vulnerabilities and create closeness, between two people. But on reflection, these 36 questions can be quite powerful for creating closeness and intimacy with yourself. Here are three questions from this article, one question from each set:

1. If you could change anything about the way you were raised, what would it be?

2. Is there something that you've dreamed of doing for a long time? Why haven't you done it?

3. Complete this sentence: "I wish I had someone with whom I could share . . ."

While all 36 questions within the article are geared toward asking someone else, you can easily modify the wording, to boomerang the question back onto yourself. The point in highlighting this popular study and article is to show that the way we build connection and intimacy with others can also be used to build connection and intimacy with self. Bottom-line: one simple tool for (self) discovery is questions—good questions—and answering them, authentically. The journey of self-inquiry remains throughout life, and your answers to questions may change and evolve over time.

Self-inquiry is a powerful tool for self-knowing, and building a strong intrapersonal relationship with yourself. Having a strong relationship with self benefits all other aspects of life—money and relationships with others included.

> *"Your own self-realization is the greatest service you can render the world."*
> —*Sri Ramana Maharshi*

Intuition

Self-knowing is a great friend of intuition, and vice versa. Intuition is inner knowledge, or knowing, that is innate and that doesn't come from a place of cognition or thinking. Intuition isn't a byproduct of rationale or reasoning; it just simply is. Whereas self-knowing relies on reflective thinking, *and* intuition. Some questions and decisions in life are best answered through intuition, while others may be best approached with a combination of self-knowing (mind) and intuition (heart).

What Are Relationships with Others?

One of the most profound (collective) realizations during the pandemic, was the value of relationships with others. Lockdowns had us recognizing the significance of gathering and connecting, as we sat in solitude and reflected. Healthy human connection makes us happier, and connection is built through shared experiences and conversation. This we know. Relationships require relating. Connecting and relating with others is accessed through sharing attention, listening intently, finding points of commonality, and being authentic; essentially, the same tools for accessing connectivity with self. With time, energy, and intentionality, meaningful relationships emerge.

Your relationship with self, your beliefs, thoughts, and emotions, color the interactions you have with others. Your natural disposition is to interpret the world through the prism of your understanding of self, which is why having a healthy foundation/concept of self is so essential. Interpretation of self reflects back in the interpretation of others (their action and words). Your beliefs, thoughts, emotions, decisions, and actions shape the quality of your relationship with others.

The quality of your relationship with others determines the quality of your life. Many of us are now carving out more time to prioritize relationships, thereby redefining relational priorities. Along this same thread, the Jewish tradition of Shabbat supports exactly this. Shabbat is the Jewish day of rest, on the seventh day of each week—Saturday. The intention is rest and reprieve from work, and to spend time with family and friends. Friday night Shabbat dinners are a time to intentionally gather, connect, and bond, all the while leaving cell phones out of the experience.

I've had the pleasure of participating in many Shabbat dinners, despite not being Jewish. One experience, in particular, really stands out in my mind—as it relates to the wealth of relationships. Here's the story. During the summer of 2021, a group of friends and I rented a house in the Hamptons. The euphoria of a summer excursion together, on the heels of 2020, was such a breath of fresh air. Toward the end of our stay, a dear friend in New York City texted me suggesting I come into the city that night (a Friday night), to join a "special" Shabbat dinner. Operating on intuition alone, I decided to get myself on the bus and journey into the city for a dinner I knew nothing about. Logically, this decision didn't make sense, because I was already in such a special setup in the Hamptons. Nonetheless, I arrived at the host's home, and noticed familiar faces—friends, and another familiar face—Esther Perel. This was a very special Shabbat dinner. The Queen of Relationships herself, Esther Perel, facilitated vulnerable conversation during dinner, through a series of questions. We went around the table, Jeffersonian style, providing deep answers to deep questions. The connection, the bonding, the vulnerability between all guests was so deeply enriching. We sat around a dinner table, passing potatoes, and also passing reflections of self. The relationships developed during this special dinner experience remain near and dear to my heart, thereby adding to the quality of my life.

> *"People organize their brains with conversation. If they don't*
> *have anyone to tell their story to, they lose their minds."*
> —*Jordan Peterson*

Relationships with others are built on shared values, experiences, and conversations. We discussed the significance of shared values and experiences, so let's now focus on *conversation*. Conversation is the interactive communication between two (or more) people, which builds a bridge between self and others. Conversations are an important form of socialization. Naturally, the types of conversations available between you and your children are different from those between you and your significant other. But the deeper you can go, within contextual reason, the better. The wonderful thing about real-time conversation is its efficiency. This may sound cold at first blush, but what I mean by this is that the feedback loop is instant. In a Forbes Business Development Council article, I wrote, "There is no substitute for free-flowing, real-time conversation. It's both raw and efficient, which is paramount for building meaningful connections with others in our increasingly fast-paced world."[3]

Through free-flowing conversation, we share and receive: time, energy, information, and knowledge. The benefit of which is real-time building of connection (or perhaps the unraveling of connection—that's possible, too). The quality of connection is based on the quality of conversing, and, of course, the quality of the company you keep. Therefore, it's wise to select and keep supportive and inspiring people in your orbit; those who positively contribute to your evolution. Bear in mind that support, inspiration, and positive contribution doesn't always come in the form of smiley faces, but sometimes in the form of hard truths.

The other day, a friend referred to someone as an "expander," and I thought that was really well put. An "expander" is someone who expands you: your vision, your aspirations, your knowledge, your confidence—whatever the case may be. Equally, it's important to positively contribute to those around you, expanding their lives for the better, too. Maybe this wears the cloak of mentorship. Or perhaps this folds into the principles of charity; in other words, generosity and helpfulness. Charity is the giving of both monetary or non-monetary value; of both tangible and intangible support.

> *"The effect you have on others is the most valuable currency there is."*
> —*Jim Carrey*

Relationships and Technology

Technology gives conversations the optionality to move from the dinner table to digital text. These days, we're connecting with others based on relevancy versus (just) proximity, because of technological advancements and societal shifts. It used to be that people would interact with those within their neighborhood, perhaps those they bartered with. But technology expanded the reach of relationships, just as it did for economies. Technology enabled social decentralization with the introduction of the telephone, internet, email, cell phone, and text messages. These advancements led to the increased reach and frequency of communication, with those down the street and with those in faraway places. It used to be that community was based on proximity, whereas now community is based on relevancy, too.

As mentioned in Chapter 2, I remember receiving my first text message from then-boyfriend, who wanted to share that he missed me (after I moved 1,300 miles away). The ability to share sentiments at any given time, peer-to-peer, regardless of geography, is quite profound. Along with emails and text messages came the electronic permanence of communication. This leads us to consider the permanence and gravity of words, particularly when allotted 160 characters per SMS text message, or 280 characters per Tweet. Both from the messenger and recipient's standpoint, the crafting and interpretation, respectively, of short form communication is becoming more frequent. Further, texting etiquette continues to evolve. Fold in emojis, and we now have more information on the sender's affect.[4]

Subjective interpretation will always exist in communication with others, whether over the dinner table or via digital text. We map our beliefs, thoughts, and emotions onto the interpretation of others' communications, which is why relationship with self impacts relationships with others. This is also why masterful communication is such a value-add, because it fosters trust and therefore healthy relationships. As Stephen M. R. Covey's book title suggests, relationships move "at the speed of trust."[5]

> *"Associate with people who are likely to improve you."*
> —*Seneca*

Here's another point to consider, speaking of subjectivity, relationships, and technology. People, regardless of age, now have access to the same information and tools (via technology) for personal-development purposes. That said, each person has the power to cultivate self-knowing and work knowledge, on their own accord, which might be sooner or later than standard. Young adults can explore topics outside of a high school or college curriculum. This supports deeper self-knowing and specialization, sooner. Plus, the ability to share knowledge and interact with others across age groups has made relating across cohorts more commonplace. This has an impact on relating and dating. This also has an impact in the professional arena, where younger leaders are stepping into the shoes of seniority, and vice versa.

Relationship Capital™

I describe *relationship capital*™ as "an intangible, super-asset that is foundational to all progress" in a *New York Times* article titled "For Elite? Yes. Ostentatious? Yes. But Also Effective."[6] Additionally, I describe relationship capital in another article as "an intangible asset that is built up over time, between two people when understanding and trust are present and growing."[7] Relationship capital is important for all types of relationships, both professional and personal. A wealth of relationship capital in business relationships can lead to better career opportunities, and in personal relationships can lead to people being there for you in good times and bad.

> *"Friends and good manners will carry you where money won't go."*
> —*Margaret Walker*

Relationships and Money

Relationships and money—an interesting topic and one that can be approached from many different angles. Building on all that we've explored thus far, let's blend the following together: the millennial cohort, technology, dating, marriage, and money.

Chapter 2 detailed the tailwinds and the headwinds for millennials, for purposes of reimaging and redefining wealth. Using a generational classification was a helpful, analytic construct, which we'll use again here, to discuss the ways in which we are revisiting relationships and money. One millennial theme is delaying the traditional hallmarks of adulthood: getting married, purchasing a home, and/or having a child. To reiterate, more than half of millennials are not married, and those who are married, got married later in life (relative to generations prior).[8] Fewer than half of millennials are home-owners.[9] A little more than half of millennial women have given birth, and those who did, did so later on in life (relative to generations prior).[10] These adulthood delays are largely a consequence of financial woes.

Technology

These adulthood delays suggest millennials are dating more during their life-time (relative to generations prior)—powered by online dating. Dating apps, specifically, have become a staple in millennial dating.[11] This makes absolute sense when you consider the fact that millennials are indeed, digital natives. Therefore, they are comfortable starting and building relationships online. Despite the absence of meta-communication (body language, facial expressions, etc.), people are able to bond, even flirt, all via text. This illustrates the evolving sophistication of digital communication. It also helps that we no longer have to triple click a key, just to arrive at the letter C for example; we now have keyboards, with one key dedicated to each letter of the alphabet. Online dating etiquette is of interesting consideration for those looking for love. Now, eligible suitors are leading with digital, instead of dinner. And per-haps, even leading with relevancy, instead of proximity (especially given the nomadic lifestyles many millennials are adopting).

There's plenty of data available shedding both positive and negative light on dating apps. Despite varying opinions on dating apps, one thing is for sure: these apps are creating societal shifts, which also permeate into other areas of life, too. Just like any tool, it's how you use it that matters, and that power is in the hand of the user. The proliferation of dating apps was supercharged during the pandemic, for obvious reasons. Social distancing brought us closer to connecting digitally. Among dating app users, 71% said they logged in more during the pandemic.[12] Those who were not open to online dating before, found themselves swiping left and right during the pandemic. Among US adults, 36% have used an online dating platform, which is up from 29% pre-pandemic (2018).[13]

For the 64% of you who don't need, or want, to explore the world of online dating, here's some quick insight into how these applications work. Essentially, you upload pictures and information about yourself into your profile—basically, branding yourself with dating in mind. Some profiles are more authentic than others. The dating apps prompt you to offer personal information by asking you questions like what's your age, gender, location, and dating preferences. Some apps ask if you have/want kids, or how often you drink socially. Other questions/information relate to religious orientation or the type of relationship you're looking for. This information serves as a filter, for others searching for their perfect match (and vice versa). This means we're selecting soulmates based on micro-bites of information and largely—pictures. In 2021, Tinder was the most downloaded dating app, followed by Bumble.[14]

Dating: The Paradox of Choice

As we know from experience, or as we can imagine, online dating creates the paradox of choice. In 2004, American psychologist Barry Schwartz popularized the concept of the *paradox of choice*, in his book: *The Paradox of Choice: Why More Is Less*.[15] This concept represents the phenomenon that it becomes really difficult to decide and choose, when we are faced with so many options. This concept was initially applied to consumer choices: "The paradox of choice stipulates that while we might believe that being presented with multiple options actually makes it easier to choose one that we are happy with, and thus increases consumer satisfaction, having an abundance of options actually requires more effort to make a decision and can leave us feeling unsatisfied with our choice. When the number of choices increases, so does the difficulty of deciding which is best. Instead of increasing our freedom to have what we want, the paradox of choice suggests that having too many choices actually limits our freedom."[16]

Have you ever logged into Netflix with the intention of watching a show or a movie, and ended up spending 30+ minutes just scrolling through the options only to find yourself closing out Netflix and going to bed instead? This is an example of choice overload, which is similar to information overload. Stressful. And unfulfilling.

Coming back to relationships, the paradox of choice holds true for dating, as well. In the search for the one, we're inundated with options of many. As it turns out, the fear of missing out applies to both experiences and dating; the fear that there may be another, better, romantic match on the other side of a few more (dating app) swipes.

High standards are important, especially when considering your life partner. As Esther Perel says, "when you pick a partner, you pick a story." And this story happens to be the story of your life, which is not trivial. Therefore, dating should be approached with a healthy dash of reality (which is not easy for me to say, as a dreamy romantic). Dating experts suggest letting go of the fantasy of perfection, of the fairytale, and especially what you see on social media. Sometimes we become married to the (artificial) concept of relationships by virtue of what we see on Instagram, for example. Hashtag "couple goals." These facades can warp our sense of reality. The bottom line is that despite the abundance of dating options available, unlocked by dating apps, we should really honor the process of dating from a lens of humanity, and perhaps humility.

We may also see the paradox of choice play out in friendships. Those looking to achieve more influence or status, for example, may optimize and maximize their options by choosing friends who will help them climb up the proverbial social ladder. Choose wisely—your friends but also your motives. After all, values and reputation are so important to your quality of life and the fabric of society. Relationships, like money, should be approached with the utmost care, to preserve and grow their value. Although, if you lose money, you can make it back. The same isn't necessarily true for relationships.

One final thought, as it relates to relationships and optionality. Some may optimize relationships for self-interested reasons, eyeing the next rung on the social ladder, perhaps at the expense of others. While all relationships include exchange, transactional relationships feel more like a business deal, an approach typically reserved for commerce. A transactional relationship may even turn asymmetrical, where one person gets more than they give—continuously. Culture calls this a toxic relationship. On the other hand, we know that relating is required for relationships, and relating is often carried out through exchange—exchange of conversation, needs, and wants. Healthy relational exchange represents the energy exchange between two people and also preserving the integrity of that exchange. Satisfying relationships require fair exchange (not one-sided, self-oriented exchange),[17] in which two people come together sharing a high-minded goal. That said, I'd be remiss not to mention the fact that marriages used to be more transactional in nature than they are today.

Marriage and Money

The definition and history of marriage deserves a book of its own, along with how people are reimaging and redefining what marriage means within our current relational paradigm. But alas, for our conversation on the value of relationships, we'll take a flash look at the evolution of marriage over the centuries.

There's a relationship between marriage and money, a relationship that's evolved over time. During antiquity, a wife's family paid a dowry (aka money, property, etc.) to a husband's family at the time of marriage. This is a clear example of the relationship between money and marriage in ancient times.

Progressing past dowry, marriage was a way of forming strategic alliances, for purposes of diplomatic and economic ties.[18] One person married another, forming an alliance between families, paving the way for a productive trading relationship. "This all changed with the differentiation of wealth."[19] As economies and wealth scaled, so did the interest in marrying into families of similar or greater wealth. Up until this point, marriage was largely transactional, because both parties (sides) had an understanding of what the other would get from the union. Consent by the two individuals marrying was of little concern or reflection; what was important, was the strategic and economical partnership formed. Marriage was really a family affair, meaning the benefits were for the family rather than for the individual specifically. However, the shift to individuation in marriage began when a monk planted the seed of *consent to marriage* in a canon law textbook in the year 1140.[20]

Gratin, a Benedictine monk, brought the element of consent into the marriage equation. Gratin asserted that each individual should give their verbal consent to consummate a marriage, which created a marital bond.[21] These new rules, forming the foundation of marriage policies in the 12th century, were intended to address the changing social landscape of marriage.[22] Marriage continued to change, evolving into a sacrament (a Catholic rite, deemed very important to the religion).[23] Ultimately, the individual became the focus in marriage, making vows to one another, and deciding whether they would marry for strategic alliances, economics, and/or love. Lastly, an individual's promise can be broken, thus ushering in divorce. Divorce via legal process became available starting in 1858.[24]

In 2020, the title of a *Wall Street Journal* article read "U.S. Marriage Rate Plunges to Lowest Level on Record; Strained finances have Americans forming households without tying the knot."[25] This article title sums up a lot of what's going on with marriage and money these days. Strained finances are impacting millennials (as we know), and middle-class Americans, which is a large reason why these demographics are delaying marriage. The societal importance of marriage is also strained, which may be a cause or effect for this cultural shift. Although, wealthy Americans, both in finance and in education, are still tying the knot, which supports the narrative that the institution of marriage is becoming more of a luxury.[26] The median wealth of married millennials is four times more than that of couples who live together but aren't married.[27] The relationship between marriage and money is alive and well, although now, people are delaying or denying marriage due to lack of money, rather than marrying for money.

History shows us the shift from marrying for the benefit of the family, to marrying for the benefit of the individual. Marital consent and personal vows led the way, as individuals took over the reins in their matrimonial decisions. In the years that followed, individualistic culture started strengthening. Individualistic cultures (versus collective cultures) are cultures that prioritize the needs of the individual over the needs of the group.[28] This type of culture tends to emphasize the importance of personal achievement, success, and financial gain. Plus, layer in the increasing number of woman going to college and participating in the workforce, resulting in more men and women pursuing their own concept of self-actualization, which often includes making money. And this makes absolute sense, because money is a necessity that affords us security, freedom, and choice (all of which are value-adds in marriage).

Individuation may correlate to the delaying of marriage as people prioritize a combination of money, health, experiences, knowledge, status, and influence ahead of tying the knot.[29] Said differently, people are perhaps not redefining the *what*, but rather the *when*, of marriage. There's a shift in viewing marriage as a capstone, versus a cornerstone or milestone in life. For some people this is a decision out of necessity, and for others a decision out of priority. Either way, the relationship between marriage and money still exists, yet for different reasons. This comes full circle, with P1, the *Wealth of Money and Investment*.

> *"It is only with the heart that one can see rightly; What's essential is invisible to the eye."*
> —Antoine de Saint-Exupéry

Part III

There's an apparent theme woven throughout the *5 Principles of Invisible Wealth*, and that's the rise of personalization and individuation. We saw this in the way that we make, spend, and invest money (P1). We also saw this theme at play in the way we manage our health, and quality of life (P2). Next, the knowledge we acquire and the status and influence we hold are all specific to the individual (P3). Plus, everyone experiences life differently, based upon the decisions they make with their time and energy (P4). Finally, your relationship with self is the most important relationship you'll ever have (P5). To put it neatly: when it comes to value and wealth, everything is personal.

> *"Yesterday I was clever, so I wanted to change the world. Today I am wise, so I am changing myself."*
>
> —*Rumi*

In Part I, we dove into the definition of wealth, the technological advancements during the millennial years, and our current, dynamic landscape. Part II introduced and explored the *5 Principles of Invisible Wealth*. Now, in Part III, we bring this abstraction into action, by using a set of instructions called the *personal wealth algorithm*. This algorithm provides guidance for defining your concept of wealth (aka your wealth goal), so that it fits snugly with your values. After defining your concept of wealth, we'll then consider the renewable resources available to achieve your wealth goal. The *personal wealth algorithm* provides a way to organize your bouquet of values into an ideal arrangement, which renewable resources help to water and grow.

Chapter 10
Personal
Wealth Algorithm

Chapter 1 started with a simple question: *What is wealth?*
To answer this question, we engaged first principles thinking, which is a critical thinking model that requires the breaking down of a concept, idea, or problem into its most fundamental parts. With our critical thinking hat on, we turned to the etymology of *wealth*, to understand the definitional roots of the word, the genesis of the word. From there, we boiled down the concept of wealth into its most fundamental parts, so we could reason and build up from there. To do so, we looked at the fundamentally familiar aspects of wealth, through a refreshed lens, that is, the 5 *Principles of Invisible Wealth*. These five principles embody the multifaceted definition of wealth, which is both evergreen and ever-evolving. These principles, plus your individual values, are the key considerations to answering the more specific question: *What's your wealth?*

This chapter introduces, and practically applies, the *personal wealth algorithm*. This algorithm, or set of instructions, is a framework for redefining wealth, so it fits snuggly with your values and goals.

> *"Philosophical sophistication, it's very useful because it orients you properly."*
>
> —*Jordan Peterson*

The Relationship Between Principles, Values, and Wealth

Within the context of wealth, the relationship between principles and values answer the question: *What's your wealth*? With this in mind, let's define both principles and values.

Principles are collective, objective truths that are unchanging and permanent, whereas *values* are individual, subjective truths that are changeable and malleable.[1] Principles transcend the individual, whereas values are specific to the individual. Principles are nondebatable, whereas values are debatable. That said, the *5 Principles of Invisible Wealth* remain objective and unchanging, whereas your values relating to wealth are subjective, or changeable. Principles act as the envelopes that hold (or house) your individual values. More on this later.

What you value today may be different than what you valued 2, 5, or 10 years ago, because of the subjective and changeable nature of values. And what you value today may be different than what you value 2, 5, or 10 years into the future. This is normal, particularly nowadays, given the velocity of change underway. As we well know, the genie is out of the bottle; therefore, knowing what you value, what you want, and what you wish for is a timely quest. This quest involves self-inquiry to thoughtfully craft a concept of wealth that fits snuggly with your values and wealth goals.

Through thousands of client conversations, I learned that wealth is personal. Further, wealth is relative, relative to the individual. I had clients who were holders of immense wealth who felt they had to live frugally. For example, one client had a net worth of over $40 million, but was skittish about leaving his job for fear of financial insecurity. Not only was he the holder of immense wealth, but also immense knowledge, status, and influence, with many money-making years ahead of him. I also saw the reverse: those who had way less financial means, yet spent beyond their means, ultimately placing them on track for financial disaster (if their spending habits weren't modified). It's all very fascinating, the way each person values and prioritizes differently. And this is exactly why reimaging and redefining wealth requires a personalized approach.

Collective Principles

Principles are collective, objective truths that are unchanging and permanent. Despite the collective, unchanging nature of principles, they can be viewed through a personalized lens. Here's an analogy to materialize this intangible concept into a tangible concept: assume you have a home with five rooms: a living room, a kitchen, a dining room, a bedroom, and a bathroom. These five rooms are unchanging and permanent, although the way you decide to furnish the rooms may change from time to time. The rooms represent principles, whereas the furniture represents values. The principles "house" your values. This backdrop provides a good opportunity to recap of the 5 *Principles of Invisible Wealth*, highlighting the personalization potential of each.

P1: *Wealth of Money and Investment*

When it comes to money and investment, it's always personal. The way you make, spend, save, and invest depends on your specific interests and goals. You make money differently than I make money, based on your interests, skills, and what the market will reward you for. How you decide to wield your productivity superpowers is specific to you. And what you spend your money on is also specific to you. As the saying goes, "Show me your receipts, and I'll show you what you value." Whether you're an entrepreneur or a corporate employee, the size of your cash cushion depends on your risk tolerance and financial goals. And finally, how you invest your additional monies is personal, too.

Working, generating income in excess of your expenses, affords you the ability to save and invest money. Investing today looks a lot different than it did in times past, particularly pre-internet and pre-online brokers. The empowerment of the individual is seen through the rise of the retail investor, taking investment into their own hands. More people are exploring wealth creation through the treasure trove of information and resources available, taking the reins over their financial future. The more people that take charge of their financial health, the better (for self and society). And while money and investment is largely a personal affair, there is no denying that society stands to benefit too. It is in the individual account owner's interest *and* society's interest to invest and grow money, because once the account owner acquires enough wealth for themselves, they are then more inclined to then share their wealth with others, whether it be with loved ones or loved causes—charity and philanthropy.

P2: *Wealth of Health and Quality of Life*

It doesn't get more personal than health, and quality of life, that's for sure! The saying "health is wealth" finds it's truth both in an etymological sense and a practical sense. From an etymological perspective, *wealth* was born from root words relating to health and well-being. From a practical perspective, health is foundational to both creating and enjoying wealth. The ways in which we manage our health today, looks different from times past, especially because technology is providing visibility into the invisible. Technology is providing visibility into the invisible markers of health like blood oxygen levels, heart rate levels, and REM sleep metrics. This information is captured thanks to wearables (ex: Oura ring). Further, we can now "see" doctors and specialists without really seeing them, through telehealth options. The digitization of healthcare provides X-ray vision into our health and habits, further personalizing the personal.

Visibility into your health data is a consequential, technological advancement, because it allows you to optimize your health and quality of life from an informed place. These quantitative insights have the potential to inform and support meaningful, qualitative changes—all of which are highly personal to you. Additionally, society is now embracing the totality of health to include wellness of mind, body, and spirit. We are valuing and prioritizing a more expansive concept of health, which includes intangible, invisible, health. Mental and spiritual strength is a powerful force. Your intuition will lead the way, in revealing how to best fortify and strengthen mind, body, and spirit.

P3: *Wealth of Knowledge, Status, and Influence*

There's not a single person on this planet who carries the same mosaic of knowledge as you do, or the same status and influence for that matter. Your logical and emotional mind determines what information is most valuable to you, at a given point in time. As you blend this information with your experiences and intuition, you become the bearer of new knowledge; knowledge you can share with others. You can share this knowledge for economic gain, through employment by self or others. The more specialized knowledge you acquire, the more money you can make by putting this knowledge to good use. From here, gaining social status is often a byproduct of providing value to your society, community, and peers.

The thing about status is it's relative to your society, community, and peers. What value do you provide to others? What associations, affiliations or memberships do you align with? These are all key contributors to status. Plus, elevated finances typically equate to elevated status, because you can pay your way into social circles. Further, influence is often a byproduct of your knowledge and status. Influence is also highly unique to you. How you influence others, and for what purposes, is based on your objectives and goals (for self and for others). And this is best achieved, when done— authentically and with good intention.

P4: Wealth of Time, Energy, and Experience

Time is your most valuable asset, despite never knowing how much you have. Therefore, the more authority you have over how you spend your time, the better. And only you can decide the best ways to do so. It might be helpful to calculate your monetary value of time, to provide a quantitative, analytical point of reference to shape your relationship with time. Understanding the value of your time, whether from a quantitative or qualitative perspective, impacts what you give your energy to and the experiences you seek.

With a grand premium placed on the value of time, it makes sense that you'd want to optimize it. Many technological advancements aim at saving time and energy, and when used with intention and discipline—they are absolute gems. The time and energy saved, thanks to technology, intention, and discipline, can be used for pursuing extraordinary experiences. Consider, what makes you feel alive, what stretches you, what makes you feel the vitality of being? This is highly personal. Fortunately, there are many options in the marketplace to find full expression of self through experiences. All this said, it's also up to you to find magic in the mundane moments of life, to fully appreciate the richness and totality of life. The only person who has control over this perspective is you.

P5: *Wealth of Relationships with Self and Others*

The most intimate relationship you'll ever have is with yourself, which is why the Greek maxim *"know thyself"* remains with us since antiquity. Self-inquiry is a portal into self-knowing, where you are both asking and answering the questions; playing both the white chess pieces and the black chess pieces. The importance of self-knowing and self-awareness is supremely valuable when you consider that your beliefs, thoughts, emotions, decisions, and actions all color the relationships and interactions with others. Additionally, relationships with others are also a portal into self-knowing, because there's an inherent feedback loop by way of conversation.

Taking this one step further, you get to decide who you want to surround yourself with—the quality of the company you keep. Seneca's timeless advice of *"Associate with people who are likely to improve you"* is especially noteworthy today, because technological advancements grant us the ability to connect with people based on relevancy over proximity. You can find people who are likely to improve you, regardless of whether (or not) they are living in your community. This is so powerful. While you may be faced with the paradox of choice, in friendly and romantic relationships, your relationship with self, your intuition, and your values and goals help lead the way in determining which relationships to invest in. Individuation of self may act as an elegant filter for who and what you associate with.

Individual Values

The *5 Principles of Invisible Wealth* are fundamentally familiar but deserve revisiting in light of the technological advancements and societal shifts currently underway. We just recapped the personalization potential of each principle, despite principles being collective, objective truths. As a follow-on, let's consider the individualistic nature of values.

Values are individual, subjective truths that are changeable and malleable.[2] Values are specific to the individual. Principles act as the envelopes that hold (or house) your individual values. Let's revisit the analogy of the home with five rooms. What you value, will furnish each of these rooms. Perhaps you value aesthetics over functionality, so your living room includes a beautiful couch that doesn't provide much function. The rooms represent principles, whereas the furniture represents values.

Understanding your personal values is important because your values influence your thoughts, behaviors, and decisions. Every day, you make about 35,000 remotely conscious decisions.[3] Every day, you're inundated with information, and options—constantly facing the paradox of choice. Your values act as the filters for your decisions, which helps to speed up your decision-making process and to keep your actions aligned with your values. This supports your ability to live an authentic, values-based, life. Here's a practical and metaphorical example. It is much more efficient to go to the grocery store with a list of what you want (what you value, at that point in time), versus going to the grocery store not knowing what you want. Without a list, without an understanding of what you want, you may end up walking around the grocery store aimlessly, wasting valuable time and energy. The same logic applies to walking through life. That said, it's powerful to know and understand what your values are.

Collective and Individualistic Culture

"As parents are to children, cultures are to adults."
—Jordan Peterson

With a solid understanding of collective principles and individual values, it seems fitting that we touch on collective and individualistic cultures, especially because culture can influence individual values. In the United States, we live in an individualist culture—a culture that prioritizes the individual ahead of the collective. Individualistic cultures celebrate personal achievements, success, and innovation.

The topic of the individual versus the collective was front and center during the height of the pandemic. There was much discussion as to how the (values) behavior of one, could impact the health of many. To slow the spread of the virus, the World Health Organization advised us to wear masks, to maintain social distancing, and to avoid large crowds. Different regions, countries, states, and even cities adopted this advice to varying degrees. Some cultures were highly compliant, whereas other cultures were not. Individuals in collective cultures were highly compliant (e.g., China), whereas individuals in individualistic cultures were not (e.g., Sweden). In the United States, we experienced a fractured approach to compliance/ noncompliance, because of the different subcultures within the country. Case in point: New York City's compliance was strict, whereas Miami's compliance was lax. But generally speaking, Americans were voicing their concern for the preservation of individual freedom and personal liberties.[4] Individualistic cultures prioritize values such as independence, freedom, self-expression, and self-definition.[5] The United States was founded on these core values.

Here are some quantitative insights to round out these qualitative statements. Dutch professor and researcher Professor Gert Jan Hofstede developed a cultural index that measures the individuality of each country's culture.[6] The more individualistic a culture, the more likely an individual will take care of themselves, instead of relying on the collective for support. Hofstede's findings reveal the following index numbers for the following countries; the higher the number, the more individualistic the country: United States (91), Sweden (71), China (20), and our North American neighbors, Canada (80) and Mexico (30).[7,8]

The concept of an individualistic culture versus a collective culture is dynamic, especially when you value attributes of both. I was born in Mexico (30), and spent formative years in Canada (80), and was raised in a household of Europeans (generally, much less individualistic than the United States). Years ago, my disposition swayed toward a collective orientation, rather than an individualistic orientation, so much so that there were times at the beginning of my career when I was coached to talk about myself more. This felt a bit taboo to me, based on the ideals that surrounded me growing up. That said, I became more comfortable and in fact, appreciative, of the individualistic orientation of individualistic culture. My values changed with time. And perhaps they were/are influenced by culture. I mention this as an example of how culture can impact our individual values, which is why spending the time and energy to "know thyself" is so important—to parse out your values from those around you.

Personal Wealth Algorithm

"I know of no more encouraging fact than the unquestionable ability of man to elevate his life by conscious endeavor."
—Henry David Thoreau

By now, we're quite familiar with the idea that you're wealthy when you have an abundance of what you value, and that wealth is a derivative of value(s). Therefore, the concept of wealth is subjective because individual values are subjective. The question then becomes: What are your values? This section is where the relationship between principles, values, and wealth really comes to life. It's also the section where you can roll up your sleeves and answer—*What's your wealth?*

The *personal wealth algorithm* provides a set of instructions to help you identify your wealth (goal). By definition, an algorithm provides a set of instructions, or orders of operation, to solve an algebraic expression/equation. In other words, algorithms are a series of steps to arrive at a solution. When you think back to algebra class, consider the order of operations you used to arrange and prioritize the values, variables, and functions, all for purposes of solving the algebraic expression at hand. Similarly, here are the set of instructions (order of operations) for defining your wealth:

1. Identify your top 10 values.
2. Allocate your top 10 values, among the *5 Principles of Invisible Wealth*.
3. Identify which principle holds the most values (value).

As you can see, we're using principles and values to identify goals.

Practical Application

The antiquated wealth paradigm, or narrative, relates solely to *Wealth of Money and Investment* (P1), whereas the *new wealth paradigm* relates to all *5 Principles of Invisible Wealth*. Our personal values highlight which of these principles is most important to us at a given point in time—informing how we should orient ourselves to attain a fulfilling life.

The *personal wealth algorithm* is a framework for synthesizing and organizing your reality.

Let's roll up our sleeves, and practically apply this algorithm to answer: *What's my wealth?* This is where things get fun.

First

First things, first: *Identify your top 10 values.*

It's daunting looking up to the sky or staring down at a sheet of paper, thinking *What are my values?* It's difficult to distill abstraction into a few words. For this reason, as a starting point, a quick Google search will return plenty of values for consideration. James Clear, author of *Atomic Habits*, has a great core values list.[9] On Clear's website, he lists the following 57 core values. Before reading through this list, I want to stress one thing: this is not an exhaustive list of values. Please do not limit yourself to a limited list. That said, there are 9 additional, blank boxes for you to expand this list, should you choose.

Authenticity	Achievement	Adventure
Authority	Autonomy	Balance
Beauty	Boldness	Compassion
Challenge	Citizenship	Community
Competency	Contribution	Creativity
Curiosity	Determination	Fairness
Faith	Fame	Friendships
Fun	Growth	Happiness
Honesty	Humor	Influence
Inner harmony	Justice	Kindness
Knowledge	Leadership	Learning
Love	Loyalty	Meaningful work
Openness	Optimism	Peace
Pleasure	Poise	Popularity

Recognition	Religion	Reputation
Respect	Responsibility	Security
Self-respect	Service	Spirituality
Stability	Success	Status
Trustworthiness	Wealth	Wisdom

From the wide universe of personal values, choose the 10 that reso-nate with you the most—the values with the highest vibrancy and prior-ity. These are intuitive decisions, rather than intellectual ones. Which values are authentic to you, not the people around you or the values your culture holds high. Consider the infinite universe of personal values, without limitation and without consideration for external influences. Which inspire you, excite you, and make you feel alive? This is a self-discovery exercise to "know thyself." These values become the compo-nents of your personal philosophy.

Second

Second, allocate your top 10 values, among the 5 *Principles of Invis-ible Wealth*.

In other words, after selecting 10 values, refer back to the 5 *Principles of Invisible Wealth* and fold (or house) each of your values into one principle. For example, my current values are: *authenticity, achievement, autonomy, cre-ativity, growth, knowledge, love, loyalty, meaningful work,* and *security*. Next, I'll fold these 10 values into the principle envelopes:

P1: *Wealth of Money and Investment*

   a. *Achievement*
   b. *Creativity*
   c. *Growth*

    d. *Meaningful work*
    e. *Security*

P2: Wealth of Health and Quality of Life

    a. *Authenticity*
    b. *Autonomy*

P3: Wealth of Knowledge, Status, and Influence

    a. *Knowledge*

P4: Wealth of Time, Energy, and Experiences

P5: Wealth of Relationships with Self and Others

    a. *Love*
    b. *Loyalty*

The categorization of these values, within the principle envelopes, is quite subjective. For example, someone else with the same values might place *security* under P5 or *growth* under P4. This highlights the fact that our values are subjective, both in selection and application. Further, while the 5 *Principles of Invisible Wealth* are collective, objective truths, there is still potential to personalize or customize the interpretation of each (as we saw at the beginning of this chapter).

Third

Third, identify which principle holds the most values (value).

Undoubtedly, we see most of my values fold into the P1 envelope, *Wealth of Money and Investment*. Therefore, I'm currently "solving for" P1. In other words, I'm giving primacy to P1. Now I understand which facet is in focus, within the multifaceted concept of wealth. This algorithm also reveals which aspect(s) of wealth take secondary priority, and so on. That said, you might discover that your wealth goals change if you use this algorithm in 2, 5, or 10 years from now.

Wealth Goals Change, Too

Things change. The etymology of words, the evolution of money, economies, technological advancements, societies—and wealth goals change, too.

We established that values are individual, subjective truths that are changeable and malleable. Life changes, and so do our goals; this includes our wealth goals. While each of the *5 Principles of Invisible Wealth* is unchanging and static, one principle will always have priority over the others. Let's consider a relatable example, to really crystallize the idea that values and priorities change.

Hop in a time machine, back to the year 2020, when everyone was experiencing the global pandemic. At this point in time, what aspect of wealth did you value the most? Let's consider the options, the *5 Principles of Invisible Wealth*:

P1: Wealth of Money and Investment

P2: Wealth of Health and Quality of Life

P3: Wealth of Knowledge, Status, and Influence

P4: Wealth of Time, Energy and Experiences

P5: Wealth of Relationships with Self and Others

Presumably, most of us valued our health, so we focused on *Wealth of Health and Quality of Life* (P2). During this time, nearly everything we did was to solve for the preservation and optimization of health. For those fortunate enough, work moved home via Zoom. We spent money on an array of vitamins and wearables to measure blood oxygen levels. We were calling our highly valued doctors for guidance. All the information we took in related to the virus; the more knowledge we had, the better. Time and energy was spent managing stress, perhaps through online meditation or through a newly purchased Peloton. And all conversations with friends and family moved from the dinner table to digital text or talk—experiences included.

During this time, supreme priority was placed on P2, so much so that the goal of maintaining and fortifying health influenced all behaviors. This is not to say that health is not typically important or prioritized, but during the pandemic, it took primacy.

Now let's consider how your values may have impacted your approach to solving for *Wealth of Health* (P2). Using the archetypal values of an individualistic culture, perhaps *freedom of choice* was the value underpinning your decisions during the pandemic. Health took primacy, and you wanted to manage the risk of contracting the virus in a way that allowed you freedom. Taking this one step further, what constitutes freedom to you may be different from what constitutes freedom to your neighbor. Alternatively, using the archetypal values of a collective culture, perhaps *responsibility toward others* was the value underpinning your decisions during the pandemic, to the detriment of your personal freedom. Health took primacy, and you wanted to manage the risk in a way that was beneficial for the collective, and yourself.

While the *Wealth of Health and Quality of Life* (P2) was the ultimate goal, the values folding into the P2 envelope were driving your behavior and decisions (relating to this goal). Values drive decisions. To reiterate a point made earlier, values help speed up the decision-making process.

In this example, the principle of *Wealth of Health and Quality of Life* (P2) was the ultimate goal. Within the context of wealth, the principle of health is a collective, objective truth that is unchanging and permanent, meaning that while health was the ultimate goal during the pandemic, that's not to say that it isn't always important. Further, in this example, we explored two different individual personal values. The first personal value was personal freedom, which is an individual, subjective truth that is changeable and malleable, meaning that while freedom was the core value in this context, it may not be the core value in another context (or principle). The second personal value was responsibility toward others, which is also an individual, subjective truth that is changeable and malleable. For purposes of this example, regardless of which core value is most aligned to you, we can see that each appropriately folds into the principle of *Wealth of Health and Quality of Life* (P2), influencing behavior.

After applying the *personal wealth algorithm*, and discovering your wealth goal, the question then becomes—how do you best achieve it?

> *"If you want to live a happy life, tie it to a goal, not to people or things."*
> —*Albert Einstein*

Chapter 11
Personal, Renewable Resources

Resources beget resources.

Money is a resource; health is a resource; knowledge, status, and influence are resources; time, energy, and experiences are resources; and relationship with self and others are resources. We organize our decisions and our lives, around attaining and sharing these resources. Whatever you do, at any given moment, expresses what you value—and by extension, your concept of wealth. In order to attain these valuable resources, you must use your own *personal, renewable resources*.

Renewable resources are replenished and regenerated, with time. The concept of renewable resources is often associated with the environment—think renewable energy, for instance. But the concept of renewable resources also applies to the individual. In this chapter, we'll explore how your own personal, renewable resources can help you in attaining your wealth goal(s), further building on the *5 Principles of Invisible Wealth*, and the *personal wealth algorithm* framework.

The Relationship Between Environmental and Personal, Renewable Resources

First, have you heard the saying: "she/he is a force of nature"? It's a saying used for describing a person who has an incredible amount of energy and influence, which comes from within. This idiom maps the qualities of worldly nature, onto the individual's nature. That said, individuals can carry the same powerful attributes as nature.

Second, consider the saying "it's in her/his nature," as an example of the similarities between environmental and personal attributes.

Third, we also see the blending together of worldly nature and individual nature in the term *Mother Nature*. Mother Nature is considered the source and guiding force behind all living beings and resources of the world, much the same as a mother is to her child. From these three examples, we realize how our language and culture recognize the fact that worldly, environmental resources are very similar to individual, personal resources. In fact, in some sense, they are one and the same.

Additionally, we've even seen the personification of nature in pop culture, through characters like the environmentalist superhero, Captain Planet. *Captain Planet* was a TV show that aired in the 1990s. This TV show was about a superhero who represented the five worldly elements: earth, wind, water, fire, and heart. Captain Planet was known for calling in his five "Planeteers," who each represented one of the five elements. The superhero called in his Planeteers to help save the world from environmental harm. The motto was "By your powers combined, I am Captain Planet!" This TV show brought awareness to environmental issues and also inspired a new generation to be change makers for the planet.[1]

Environmental, Renewable Resources

The environmental movement started in the 1970s. This movement is a political and social movement that addresses environmental issues. These issues include anything from pollution to the depletion of finite, natural resources—the issues Captain Planet and his Planeteers were striving to solve for. Those advocating to solve these issues believe that public policy and individual behavior can help in curtailing the damage caused to mother earth. There are many environmental issues searching for solutions, but for purposes of our exploration, we'll focus on the topic of renewable energy as a precursor to the personal, renewable resources discussion.

Non-renewable Energy

To understand what renewable energy is, let's understand what it's not. *Non-renewable energy* is a finite resource that cannot be replenished at the speed in which it is consumed.[2] These resources are extracted from the earth. Examples of non-renewable energy include:

1. Oil (aka petroleum)
2. Natural gas
3. Coal
4. Nuclear, electric power

We are familiar with these resources and know them well, because they fuel (most) cars, planes, and kitchen stoves. They also give us light (electricity), among many other daily necessities. About 80% of the world's energy is consumed by using nonrenewable resources, also called fossil fuels.[3]

There are two issues with this. One, the fact that the world's energy consumption is so heavily reliant on finite resources is scary. And if we fold in economics, supply/demand dynamics dictate that these resources will become more expensive over time, because there will be less of them; the more scarce a valuable resource is, the more expensive it becomes. Two, the burning of these fossil fuels (to create energy) releases carbon dioxide (CO_2) into the atmosphere, and carbon dioxide into the air is not great. CO_2 emissions negatively impact our skies and our oceans. For this reason, non-renewables are considered unsustainable because of their finite nature and the damage they cause the environment. For these two reasons, environmentalists are advocating for new ways to supply energy to the world. This is where renewable resources come into play.

Before pivoting over to renewable resources, another related example of non-renewable resources is gold. In Chapter 1, we explored how and why gold is (historically) such a valuable asset. Gold is a finite resource, sourced from the earth, which is *one* of the reasons why it's so valuable—the scarcity element.

Non-renewable resources certainly provide value, but the question is, at what cost?

Renewable Energy

Renewable energy is an infinite resource that can be replenished at the speed in which it is consumed.[4] Captain Planet gave us a preview of these resources, but here are the five main examples of renewable energy (and their sources)[5]:

1. Solar energy (from sun)
2. Geothermal energy (from earth)
3. Wind energy (from wind)
4. Biomass energy (from plants)
5. Hydropower energy (from water)

In 2021, the United States received 87% of its energy from non-renewable sources, while 13% came from renewable sources.[6] This was a record year, in terms of how much renewable energy was consumed within the United States.[7] Increasing the use of renewables to supplement non-renewables would be advantageous for a couple of reasons. First, it would reduce the world's reliance on finite resources. Second, it would reduce the amount of carbon dioxide released into the atmosphere, for the benefit of our skies and oceans, and, ultimately, for society.

Both policy and people are behind the environmental movement, with a focus on transitioning away from our reliance on non-renewable energy and over to the reliance on renewable energy. Our current age-old energy infrastructure plus corporate and political interests make this transition clunky. Furthermore, the transition costs money, lots of money. Plus, there are a lot of trade-off considerations to account for. But generally speaking, we are invested in optimizing energy for the environment, just the same as we are interested in optimizing energy for ourselves.

A final point on renewable resources, which I would be remiss not to mention, is the fact that some are intangible. As you can see from the renewable resources listed earlier, solar energy and wind energy are sourced from intangible forces. This reiterates the point that so much power is derived from intangible, invisible forces. Further, intangible assets have the potential to ultimately reveal themselves tangibly. For example, solar transportation, getting you from point A to point B, or an electric stove cooking you a nutritious meal.

Personal, Renewable Resources

The concept of renewable resources is associated with the environment, but the concept also maps onto the individual; the world has renewable resources, and so do you. Renewable resources are sourced from within the earth, just the same as renewable resources are sourced from within you. You are a force of nature; it's in your nature, just like Mother Nature. Your renewable resources are sourced from within you, and can be replenished and regenerated. Grit, creativity, determination, and commitment are all examples of *personal, renewable resources.*

Attaining Your Wealth Goals

The *5 Principles of Invisible Wealth*, paired with the *personal wealth algorithm* framework, help in synthesizing and prioritizing your wealth goals. Thereafter, *personal, renewable resources* empower you to attain those wealth goals.

After identifying your wealth goal, then you can visualize and feel what it would be like to attain this goal. What does achieving your wealth goal look like, in your mind's eye? With your invisible paintbrush, paint the picture. Further, what does it feel like to attain this goal, to have this type of wealth? Pairing the visual with the feeling allows them to play together. Identifying your goal is one thing, visualizing and feeling it's achievement is another. Taking this one step further, writing down what this achievement looks and feels like, is telling. After all, words architect our lives. Define your goal, visualize your goal, feel your goal, and write it down. You're the creator. Each aspect of wealth holds infinite potential.

> *"Edit your life frequently and ruthlessly. It's your masterpiece after all."*
> —*Nathan M. Morris*

In the previous chapter, we used aspect of wealth the *personal wealth algorithm* to identify and prioritize your wealth goals. Then, for sake of conversation, we took my situation and practically applied this algorithm. Together, we discovered that the *Wealth of Money and Investment* (P1) takes primacy for me, right now. After leaving my job, becoming part of the Great Resignation statistics, I'm now fully committed to reimagining and redefining P1. This I know. But how do I achieve this goal? With the help of my *personal, renewable resources.*

As John Dewey, an American philosopher and psychologist, once said, "A problem well put is half solved." Once your wealth goal—your destination—is well put, then your renewable resources fuel the journey to solution. As we saw in Chapter 6, daily decisions decide our lives—one thought at a time, one decision at a time. The quality of your thoughts, and decisions, matter. Once you know what goal, or destination, to aim for, your thoughts and decisions calibrate accordingly. Your internal GPS knows the way. We also saw in Chapter 6, that the game of life is full of twists and turns, unforeseen and unexpected variables. While you might miss an exit on the road to your destination, your internal GPS will always recalibrate so long as you're committed to reaching the destination.

When you think about the nature of your *personal, renewable resources,* consider your strengths, the things you're good at, and what you enjoy doing. For some, imagination and creativity are the resources most accessible from within, whereas for others it's discipline and tenacity. Or perhaps it's using mental resources, whereas for others it's using physical resources. Throughout life, we continuously mine and cultivate these gems from within. This happens through learning new information, from experiences (both the ordinary and the extraordinary), and through conversations with friends. But ultimately, these gems are polished through conversations with self. This is where the Greek maxim "know thyself" comes back into play. Having an awareness for your attributes, your skills, your talents, your interests, and what lights you up inside, informs the *how* of achieving your (wealth) goals. This requires the quieting of the outside world, for purposes of hearing your inside world. Your inner world is more valuable than you can imagine.

After all, the largest untapped resources in the world lay within us—superpowers included.

Your Renewable Resources Are Your Superpowers

Captain Planet isn't the only one with superpowers.

Recently, I had dinner with five incredible female founders. During this dinner, one woman asked a question to the group: *What is your superpower*? Everyone paused, took a sip from their wine glass, and pondered. Then we went around the table, and each person shared her superpower, some in a personal context and others in a professional context—and sometimes the two were one and the same. For example, one founder, Sarah, said her superpower is empathy, the ability to empathize in her personal and professional life. This power is a renewable resources that comes from within, which is used to attain and share resources.

Empathy involves attributes like compassion, kindness, thoughtfulness, and relationship capital™. This superpower, these resources, are all sourced from within, and replenish and regenerate, with time. These assets are infinite, limitless, and abundant in nature, because there's no limit to the amount of empathy one can offer to self and others. Recognizing your renewable resources, your superpower (attributes, skills, talents, and interests), is largely based on your beliefs, which influence your thoughts, which then influence your decisions. Case in point, one must recognize, believe, or trust they are empathetic in order to think they are empathetic, and to then make decisions supporting this belief. My founder friend Sarah recognizes her ability to empathize with others in both a personal and professional context. If she didn't recognize, believe, or trust, in this superpower, she wouldn't think to lean into, and act on, it.

The superpower of empathy leads to establishing and building meaningful relationships as you authentically showcase your ability to offer compassion and care to others. This is an example of resources begetting resources. Sarah, an empathetic friend and superhero, wields her powers to enhance the lives of others—through genuinely stepping into the shoes of others, and understanding their situation. She enjoys using this renewable resource to achieve a *Wealth of Relationships with Self and Others* (P5).

Inside Out

"If your happiness depends upon what is happening outside of you, you will always be a slave to the external situation."

—*Sadhguru*

You can tap into your wellspring of resources at any time, and use them to fuel and achieve your (wealth) goals. These powerful resources are invisible, yet have the potential to reveal themselves, visibly.

Technological advancements and societal shifts are inviting us to rethink and reconsider what we value, and, by extension, how we define wealth. With so much going on in the outside world, the most valuable thing we can do for ourselves is to turn inward, and live from within. While technology can provide lots of distraction and noise, it can also remove lots of distraction and noise as well. Technology can take a lot of to-dos off of your plate. Consider all the time and energy saved due to online shopping, automation, access to information, and various time-saving apps. This is an absolute win for freeing up your time and energy, so you can tap into your renewable, superpowers—to do superhuman things.

Modern technology provides the (physical and mental) space, for you to use your ancient technology. Your ancient technologies include: language, intuition, inner knowledge, your spirit animal essence, and your personal, renewable resources. Modern technology also enables wider and deeper use of these ancient technologies. For example, consider how much you use language in emails, text messages, and online communication. Plus, consider how much of what you say in these communications, comes from a place of intuition or inner knowing. That said, Google might be the largest search engine in the world, but the most valuable questions can only be answered from within.

Speaking of technology, computers and people are more similar than we'd initially assume. Chapter 6 reminded us that our energy comes from the wellspring within. This energy is our processing power. *Processing power* is typically a term reserved for computer speak, when discussing the ability of computers to complete tasks. But people have *processing power* too, which gives us the ability to complete our goals. In computers, updating the software makes the system run better, improving it's processing power. In people, updating our software makes our systems run better, improving our processing superpower. Software updates find glitches (the things that aren't working) and improves upon them. We recognize glitches in our own software, or said differently, in our beliefs, thoughts, emotions, and decisions when we experience something going wrong or when we confront a challenge. Glitches or challenges, invite us to revisit our operating system and improve it. People are strengthened by pushing up against hard things (both physically and mentally). Each glitch or challenge provides the opportunity to consciously update your software; thereby, increasing your superpowers thereafter.

> *"Don't limit your challenges. Challenge your limits."*
> —*Anonymous*

External, Renewable Resources

Turning inward before turning outward is an algorithm for success. Our internal knowing guides what external knowledge to seek. That said, external, renewable resources can also help in attaining your wealth goal.

External, renewable resources elegantly complement our *personal, renewable resources*—in actualizing our wealth goal. External, renewable resources are replenished and regenerated with time, and found outside of self. Think: books, podcasts, and mentors. Books are renewable because you can always go back to them, whether the book is on your Kindle or on your book shelf at home. Podcasts are renewable because you can listen and relisten until your heart's content. And mentors are renewable resources, because they can provide you guidance and support throughout life—as long as the relationship is managed with care. Each of these resources are value-adds when aligned with your values, principles, and goals. External resources are like friends in the passenger seat, while you journey to destination P1, P2, P3, P4, or P5. Your internal GPS is on, but your friend is there to nudge you and say the exit is on the right, right after the gas station. These resources provide an additional dimension to your own.

Books, podcasts, and mentors are just a few examples of the external, renewable resources available to help you on your wealth journey. These resources provide rich information, supporting guiding journey. With goal in mind, intentionality can follow; consciously seeking and internalizing.

As we well know, there is more information available to us today than ever before. Consider the points made in Chapter 7, when we discussed the knowledge doubling curve. This is leverage. Leverage is something that helps to maximize what you already have.

In the wealth advisor seat, I would often tell my new clients that they could consider me and my team as their board of advisors. Each person on my team had a primary focus and expertise, and we would all sit around the table, viewing the client's dynamic financial landscape, with a 360-degree view. Each teammate was there to support the client, by providing his/her own expertise, at any given time. Similarly, people can adopt this same model in their personal lives. Simply put, constructing your own board of advisors. Consider the top five people you admire the most—those whose judgment you trust. Those are the people you want on your board of advisors. We naturally do this, by always calling the same friends when we have issues. But take an intentional look at who these individuals are, and perhaps consider adding to this cohort and/or constructing a board of advisors for personal matters, and a board of advisors for professional matters.

There's much to learn from other people's perspectives and experiences. First, how they make, save, spend, and invest their money. Second, how they optimize their health and quality of life. Third, how they manage their time, energy, and experiences. Fourth, how they expand their knowledge, status, and influence, for the greater good. And fifth, how they establish and grow their relationships with self and others. Further, how do others approach their principles, values, and goals? And here's a little secret, people are looking to you for inspiration on how to approach their principles, values, and goals. This is why sharing your knowledge and wisdom is so important for the benefit of others.

Where Wealth Begins

You didn't need this book to tell you that we're in the midst of a huge paradigm shift; this you already know. But perhaps this book did invite you to consciously consider what you value, and therefore how to (re)define wealth, within the *new wealth paradigm*. This new paradigm is inviting us to rethink what we value, and therefore how we define wealth, because we are wealthy when we have an abundance of what we value. Additionally, we are becoming increasingly comfortable with pegging value to intangible assets, as we fundamentally always have.

Technological advancements and societal shifts are providing the opportunity to reconceptualize so many aspects of our lives, wealth included; wealth, in every sense of the word. We are revisiting our personal finances alongside our personal philosophies. We are also revisiting financial value, and personal values. It's my hope that a holistic and authentic concept of wealth aligns you with what you value most. Define your wealth, *Invisible Wealth*.

Notes

Chapter 1

1. *Encyclopaedia Britannica Online*, s.v. "economy." Accessed October 2, 2022. https://www.britannica.com/dictionary/economy.

2. DeVita, Krystin. "First Principles Thinking Adopted from Aristotle." Jumpstart Health Investors, December 23, 2020. https://www.jumpstarthealth.co/blog-1/first-principles-thinking-adopted-from-aristotle.

3. Fridman, Lex. *Elon Musk: First Principles*. YouTube, 2018. https://www.youtube.com/watch?v=bLv9MGsUt6g.

4. *Online Etymology Dictionary*, s.v. "wealth." Accessed October 2, 2022. https://www.etymonline.com/word/wealth#etymonline_v_4871.

5. *Online Etymology Dictionary*, s.v. "weal." Accessed October 2, 2022. https://www.etymonline.com/search?q=weal.

6. *Online Etymology Dictionary*, s.v. "wealthy." Accessed October 2, 2022. https://www.etymonline.com/word/wealthy#etymonline_v_40133.

7. Online Etymology Dictionary, s.v. "commonwealth." Accessed October 2, 2022. https://www.etymonline.com/search?q=commonwealth.

8. *Merriam-Webster Online*, s.v. "wealth." Accessed October 2, 2022. https://www.merriam-webster.com/dictionary/wealth.

9. Ibid.

10. Spaulding, William C. "Commodity, Representative, Fiat, and Electronic Money" in "Money." *This Matter*. Accessed October 2, 2022. https://thismatter.com/money/banking/money.htm.

11. Amadeo, Kimberly. "Gold Standard." *The Balance*, March 17, 2022. https://www.thebalance.com/what-is-the-history-of-the-gold-standard-3306136.

12. Lioudis, Nick. "What Is the Gold Standard? Advantages, Alternatives, and History." *Investopedia*, March 4, 2022. https://www.investopedia.com/ask/answers/09/gold-standard.asp.

13. *Merriam-Webster Online*, s.v. "fiat." Accessed October 2, 2022. https://www.merriam-webster.com/dictionary/fiat.

14. Ibid.

15. "USA Inflation Rate." Inflation Rate and Consumer Price Index, September 13, 2022. https://www.rateinflation.com/inflation-rate/usa-inflation-rate/.

16. Spaulding, William C. "Money."

17. Bloomenthal, Andrew. "The Power of Electronic Money." *Investopedia*, May 31, 2022. https://www.investopedia.com/terms/e/electronic-money.asp.

18. Rodeck, David, and Benjamin Curry. "Digital Currency: The Future of Your Money." *Forbes,* April 1, 2021. https://www.forbes.com/advisor/investing/cryptocurrency/digital-currency/.

19. Ranzetta, Tim. "Question: What Percentage of the Money Supply Is in Physical Coins and Currency?" *Next Gen Personal Finance,* May 22, 2017. https://www.ngpf.org/blog/uncategorized/question-percentage-money-supply-physical-coins-currency/.

20. Nakamoto, Satoshi. "Bitcoin: A Peer-to-Peer Electronic Cash System." Bitcoin.org, October 31, 2008. https://bitcoin.org/bitcoin.pdf.

21. Ibid.

22. Wagner, Casey. "Bitcoin, Ether to Be Regulated as Commodities by CFTC, per New Senate Bill." *Blockworks*, August 3, 2022. https://blockworks.co/bitcoin-ether-to-be-regulated-as-commodities-by-cftc-per-new-senate-bill/.

23. "Divisibility: River Glossary." River Financial. Accessed October 2, 2022. https://river.com/learn/terms/d/divisibility/.

24. Ben Hur, Roy, Zachary Aron, Rakinder Sembhi, and Richard Rosenthal. "Digital Assets & CBDCs Are Here." Deloitte United States, 2022. https://www2.deloitte.com/us/en/pages/consulting/articles/digital-assets-cbdcs-and-stablecoins-digital-economy-review.html.

25. Ibid.

26. *Encyclopedia Britannica Online*, s.v. "economy." Accessed October 2, 2022. https://www.britannica.com/dictionary/economy.

27. Beggs, Jodi. "What's the Real Function of Money?" ThoughtCo., February 5, 2019. https://www.thoughtco.com/what-is-money-1147763.

28. Sharma, Rakesh. "Who Was Adam Smith?" *Investopedia*, April 11, 2022. https://www.investopedia.com/updates/adam-smith-economics/.

29. "What Is Economics?" Corporate Finance Institute, May 7, 2022. https://corporatefinanceinstitute.com/resources/knowledge/economics/what-is-economics/.

30. Smith, Adam. "An Inquiry into the Nature and Causes of the Wealth of Nations by Adam Smith." Project Gutenberg, June 1, 2002. https://www.gutenberg.org/ebooks/3300.

31. Majaski, Christina. "What Is the Invisible Hand in Economics?" *Investopedia*, August 30, 2022. https://www.investopedia.com/terms/i/invisiblehand.asp.

32. Munger, Michael. "Division of Labor, Part 1." *Adam Smith Works*, August 7, 2019. https://www.adamsmithworks.org/documents/division-of-labor-part-1.

33. Ibid.

34. Smith, "An Inquiry into the Nature and Causes of the Wealth of Nations."

35. "Internet & World Wide Web." Basu. Accessed October 3, 2022. https://basu.org.in/.

36. "Internet Growth Statistics." Internet World Stats. Accessed October 2, 2022. https://www.internetworldstats.com/emarketing.htm.

Chapter 2

1. Godbout, Ted. "Wealth Transfers to Hit $84 Trillion through 2045." National Association of Plan Advisors, January 27, 2022. https://www.napa-net.org/news-info/daily-news/wealth-transfers-hit-84-trillion-through-2045.

2. "The Ultimate List of Millennial Characteristics." Lucky Attitude, November 2, 2021. https://luckyattitude.co.uk/millennial-characteristics/.

3. Ibid.

4. Fry, Richard. "Millennials Overtake Baby Boomers as America's Largest Generation." Pew Research Center, April 28, 2021. https://www.pewresearch.org/fact-tank/2020/04/28/millennials-overtake-baby-boomers-as-americas-largest-generation/.

5. Ibid.

6. Strickland, Jonathan, and Wesley Fenlon. "10 Cool Inventions from the 1980s." HowStuffWorks, September 15, 2022. https://science.howstuffworks.com/innovation/inventions/5-cool-inventions-from-the-1980s.htm.

7. "Internet & World Wide Web." Basu. Accessed October 3, 2022. https://basu.org.in/.

8. *Wikipedia*, s.v. "mobile phone." Accessed October 3, 2022. https://en.wikipedia.org/wiki/Mobile_phone.

9. Joquita. "11 Things You Didn't Know That Were Invented in the 1980s." *80s baby*. Accessed October 3, 2022. https://www.80sbaby.org/blog-11-things-you-didnt-know-that-were-invented-in-the-1980s/.

10. Brown, Jen. "The 10 Most Influential '90s Technology Innovations." *Retropond*, April 2, 2021. https://retropond.com/10-most-influential-90s-technology-innovations/.

11. Leadem, Rose. "10 Inventions That Prove the Best Things Were Born in the 90s." *Chron.*, May 10, 2021. https://www.chron.com/business/article/10-inventions-that-prove-the-best-things-were-16163596.php.

12. Ibid.

13. "How We Started and Where We Are Today." Google. Accessed October 3, 2022. https://about.google/our-story/.

14. *Wikipedia*, s.v. "Google search." Accessed October 3, 2022. https://en.wikipedia.org/wiki/Google_Search.

15. Graf, Nikki. "Today's Young Workers Are More Likely Than Ever to Have a Bachelor's Degree." Pew Research Center, July 27, 2020. https://www.pewresearch.org/fact-tank/2017/05/16/todays-young-workers-are-more-likely-than-ever-to-have-a-bachelors-degree/.

16. The Investopedia Team. "2008 Recession: What the Great Recession Was and What Caused It." *Investopedia*, May 26, 2022. https://www.investopedia.com/terms/g/great-recession.asp.

17. *Wikipedia*, s.v. "History of Federal Open Market Committee actions." Accessed October 3, 2022. https://en.wikipedia.org/wiki/History_of_Federal_Open_Market_Committee_actions.

18. The Investopedia Team. "2008 Recession."

19. Chen, James. "What Is the Prime Rate?" *Investopedia*, September 25, 2022. https://www.investopedia.com/terms/p/primerate.asp.

20. Ibid.

21. "Mortgage Debt Outstanding, All Holders (Discontinued)." FRED, December 12, 2019. https://fred.stlouisfed.org/series/MDOAH.

22. The Investopedia Team. "What Role Did Securitization Play in the Global Financial Crisis?" *Investopedia*, August 27, 2021. https://www.investopedia.com/ask/answers/041515/what-role-did-securitization-play-us-subprime-mortgage-crisis.asp.

23. Holmes, Steven A. "Fannie Mae Eases Credit to Aid Mortgage Lending." *New York Times,* September 30, 1999. https://www.nytimes.com/1999/09/30/business/fannie-mae-eases-credit-to-aid-mortgage-lending.html?sec=&spon=&pagewanted=all.

24. Kagan, Julia. "Mortgage-Backed Securities (MBS) Definition: Types of Investment." *Investopedia*, October 28, 2021. https://www.investopedia.com/terms/m/mbs.asp.

25. *Wikipedia*, s.v. "Causes of the 2000s United States Housing Bubble." Accessed October 3, 2022. https://en.wikipedia.org/wiki/Causes_of_the_2000s_United_States_housing_bubble.

26. Timiraos, Nick. "Holding Rates Steady, Fed Plays down Worries on Low Inflation." *Wall Street Journal*, May 1, 2019. https://www.wsj.com/articles/fed-holds-rates-steady-says-spending-inflation-have-slowed-11556733726.

27. "S&P 500 Index - 90 Year Historical Chart." MacroTrends. Accessed October 3, 2022. https://www.macrotrends.net/2324/sp-500-historical-chart-data.

28. "Dow Jones - DJIA - 100 Year Historical Chart." MacroTrends. Accessed October 3, 2022. https://www.macrotrends.net/1319/dow-jones-100-year-historical-chart.

29. "S&P/Case-Shiller U.S. National Home Price Index." FRED, September 27, 2022. https://fred.stlouisfed.org/series/CSUSHPINSA.

30. "U.S. Unemployment Rate 1991–2022." MacroTrends. Accessed October 3, 2022. https://www.macrotrends.net/countries/USA/united-states/unemployment-rate.

31. Weinberg, John. "The Great Recession and Its Aftermath." Federal Reserve History, November 22, 2013. https://www.federalreservehistory.org/essays/great-recession-and-its-aftermath.

32. Ibid.

33. "10 Years Later: The Lehman Brothers Administration – Reflections and Ongoing Impact: Thought Leadership." Linklaters. Accessed October 3, 2022. https://www.linklaters.com/en-us/insights/thought-leadership/lehman-10-years/10-years-later---the-lehman-brothers-administration.

34. Lioudis, Nick. "The Collapse of Lehman Brothers: A Case Study." *Investopedia*, January 30, 2021. https://www.investopedia.com/articles/economics/09/lehman-brothers-collapse.asp.

35. "Timeline: Key Dates in the History of the Personal Computer." Reuters, January 6, 2009. https://www.reuters.com/article/us-laptop-sb/timeline-key-dates-in-the-history-of-the-personal-computer-idUKTRE50601V20090107.

36. Rich, Robert. "The Great Recession." Federal Reserve History, November 22, 2013. https://www.federalreservehistory.org/essays/great-recession-of-200709.

37. "All Employees, Total Nonfarm." FRED, September 2, 2022. https://fred.stlouisfed.org/series/PAYEMS.

38. Underwood, Angela. "30 Toys That Defined the '80s." *Stacker*, November 24, 2021. https://stacker.com/stories/3671/30-toys-defined-80s.

39. Barroso, Amanda, Kim Parker, and Jesse Bennett. "As Millennials Near 40, They're Approaching Family Life Differently Than Previous Generations." Pew Research Center's Social & Demographic Trends Project, May 27, 2020. https://www.pewresearch.org/social-trends/2020/05/27/as-millennials-near-40-theyre-approaching-family-life-differently-than-previous-generations/.

40. Cachero, Paulina, and Ella Ceron. "Why Aren't Millennials Buying Home? 4 Charts Explain." Bloomberg, March 23, 2022. https://www.bloomberg.com/news/articles/2022-03-23/why-aren-t-millennials-buying-home-4-charts-explain.

41. Barroso, Parker, and Bennett, "As Millennials Near 40.".

42. Rockeman, Olivia, and Catarina Saraiva. "Millennials Age 40 with No Home, More Debt Run out of Time to Build Wealth." Bloomberg, June 3, 2021.

43. "The Deloitte Global 2022 Gen Z and Millennial Survey." Deloitte. Accessed October 4, 2022.

44. "Distribution of Household Wealth in the U.S. since 1989." DFA: Distributional Financial Accounts. Federal Reserve, September 23, 2022. https://www.federalreserve.gov/releases/z1/dataviz/dfa/distribute/chart/.

45. Daniel, Will. "Millennials' Wealth Has More Than Doubled since the Pandemic Began." Fortune, March 22, 2022. https://fortune.com/2022/03/22/millennial-wealth-doubles-during-pandemic-9-trillion-boomers/.

46. Cook, Alex. "Millennials' Net Worth Has Doubled since Start of Pandemic." MagnifyMoney, July 25, 2022. https://www.magnifymoney.com/news/net-worth-of-millennials/.

47. Godbout, "Wealth Transfers to Hit $84 Trillion."

48. Hoffower, Hillary. "The 40-Year-Old Millennial and the 24-Year-Old Gen Zer Are in Charge of America Right Now." Business Insider, September 26, 2021. https://www.businessinsider.com/24-gen-z-trends-40-millennial-spending-changing-economy-2021-9.

Chapter 3

1. Bakhtiari, Kian. "Why Brands Need to Prepare for the Great Wealth Transfer." Forbes, August 8, 2022. https://www.forbes.com/sites/kianbakhtiari/2022/08/08/why-brands-need-to-prepare-for-the-great-wealth-transfer/?sh=5e05a7f44b81.

2. Ibid.

3. Henderson, Tim. "The Pandemic Prompted People to Move, but Many Didn't Go Far." The Pew Charitable Trusts, March 23, 2022. https://www.pewtrusts.org/en/research-and-analysis/blogs/stateline/2022/03/23/the-pandemic-prompted-people-to-move-but-many-didnt-go-far.

4. Ibid.

5. Ramani, Arjun, and Nicholas Bloom. "The Donut Effect of Covid-19 on Cities." WFH Research, May 21, 2021. https://wfhresearch.com/wp-content/uploads/2021/05/DONUT_MAY21.pdf.

6. Henderson, "The Pandemic Prompted People to Move."

7. Ang, Carmen. "Mapping the Migration of the World's Millionaires." Visual Capitalist, June 15, 2022. https://www.visualcapitalist.com/migration-of-millionaires-worldwide-2022/.

8. Villanova, Patrick. "Where High-Earning Households Are Moving—2022 Study." SmartAsset, August 4, 2022. https://smartasset.com/data-studies/where-high-earning-households-are-moving-2022.

9. "Federal Funds Rate—62 Year Historical Chart." MacroTrends. Accessed October 4, 2022. https://www.macrotrends.net/2015/fed-funds-rate-historical-chart.

10. "2020 Home Buyers and Sellers Generational Trends Report." National Associations of Realtors Research Group, March 2020. https://www.nar.realtor/sites/default/files/documents/2020-generational-trends-report-03-05-2020.pdf.

11. "2021 Home Buyers and Sellers Generational Trends Report." National Association of Realtors Research Group. Accessed October 5, 2022. https://www.nar.realtor/sites/default/files/documents/2021-home-buyers-and-sellers-generational-trends-03-16-2021.pdf.

12. "2022 Home Buyers and Sellers Generational Trends Report." National Association of Realtors Research Group. Accessed October 5, 2022. https://cdn.nar.realtor/sites/default/files/documents/2022-home-buyers-and-sellers-generational-trends-03-23-2022.pdf.

13. Wile, Rob. "Millennials Make up the Largest Share of Homebuyers in America, According to Recent Data." NBC News, April 6, 2022. https://www.nbcnews.com/business/consumer/millennial-homebuyers-now-the-largest-share-of-market-in-america-rcna22894.

14. "Spain POPULATION 2022 Data—2023 Forecast—1960–2021 Historical." Trading Economics. Accessed October 4, 2022. https://tradingeconomics.com/spain/population.

15. Fuller, Joseph, and William Kerr. "The Great Resignation Didn't Start with the Pandemic." *Harvard Business Review*, March 23, 2022. https://hbr.org/2022/03/the-great-resignation-didnt-start-with-the-pandemic.

16. Barnes, Mitchell, Lauren Bauer, and Wendy Edelberg. "11 Facts on the Economic Recovery from the COVID-19 Pandemic." Brookings, September 29, 2021. https://www.brookings.edu/research/11-facts-on-the-economic-recovery-from-the-covid-19-pandemic/.

17. Parker, Kim, and Juliana Menasce Horowitz. "Majority of Workers Who Quit a Job in 2021 Cite Low Pay, No Opportunities for Advancement, Feeling Disrespected." Pew Research Center, March 9, 2022. https://www.pewresearch.org/fact-tank/2022/03/09/majority-of-workers-who-quit-a-job-in-2021-cite-low-pay-no-opportunities-for-advancement-feeling-disrespected/.

18. Ibid.

19. Rinz, Kevin. "Did Timing Matter? Life Cycle Differences in Effects of Exposure to the Great Recession." U.S. Census Bureau, May 17, 2022. https://kevinrinz.github.io/recession.pdf.

20. "Wage Growth Tracker." Federal Reserve Bank of Atlanta. Accessed October 4, 2022. https://www.atlantafed.org/chcs/wage-growth-tracker.

21. "Unemployment Rate." FRED, September 2, 2022. https://fred.stlouisfed.org/series/UNRATE.

22. Ibid.

23. Bruner, Raisa. "The Great Resignation Fueled Higher Pay-for Everyone." *Time*, January 27, 2022. https://time.com/6143212/us-wage-growth-record-high/.

24. Parker and Menasce Horowitz, "Majority of Workers Who Quit a Job in 2021 Cite Low Pay."

25. Ibid.

26. Fox, Michelle. "The Great Resignation Has Changed the Workplace for Good. 'We're Not Going Back,' Says the Expert Who Coined the Term." CNBC, May 10, 2022. https://www.cnbc.com/2022/05/10/-the-great-resignation-has-changed-the-workplace-for-good-.html.

27. Tardi, Carla. "Don't Let Your Animal Spirits Influence Your Important Decisions." *Investopedia*, May 24, 2021. https://www.investopedia.com/terms/a/animal-spirits.asp.

28. Wolf Herd, Whitney. "Bumble's Founder and CEO Whitney Wolfe Herd Talks Building Bumble—and Fighting for Gender Equality." Bumble Buzz. Accessed October 4, 2022. https://bumble.com/en-us/the-buzz/a-letter-from-whitney-wolfe-herd-founder-and-ceo.

29. Ingalls, Sam. "What Is Digital Darwinism?" *Webopedia*, April 27, 2021. https://www.webopedia.com/definitions/what-is-digital-darwinism/.

30. "2022 M&A: Continued Strength Post Peak." Morgan Stanley, January 14, 2022. https://www.morganstanley.com/ideas/mergers-and-acquisitions-outlook-2022-continued-strength-after-record.

31. Ibid.

Chapter 5

1. McWhinney, James. "The Demise of the Defined-Benefit Plan." *Investopedia*, July 18, 2022. https://www.investopedia.com/articles/retirement/06/demiseofdbplan.asp.

2. Zhou, Luisa. "2022 Side Hustle Statistics: The Ultimate List." *Luisa Zhou* (blog), June 3, 2022. https://www.luisazhou.com/blog/side-hustle-statistics/.

3. Ibid.

4. "Adobe 'Future of Creativity' Study: 165m+ Creators Joined Creator Economy since 2020." Adobe, August 25, 2022. https://news.adobe.com/news/news-details/2022/Adobe-Future-of-Creativity-Study-165M-Creators-Joined-Creator-Economy-Since-2020/default.aspx.

5. *Wikipedia*, s.v. "creator economy." Accessed October 4, 2022. https://en.wikipedia.org/wiki/Creator_economy.

6. "Adobe 'Future of Creativity' Study."

7. Ibid.

8. Pop-Andonov, Neda. "The Creator Economy Market Size in 2022." Influencers Club, June 14, 2022. https://influencers.club/2022/06/14/creator-economy-market-size/.

9. "Adobe 'Future of Creativity' Study."

10. *Wikipedia*, s.v. "Web3." Accessed October 4, 2022. https://en.wikipedia.org/wiki/Web3.

11. Kannan, Sreekanth. "What Is Web3?—Definition from Techopedia." *Techopedia*, May 18, 2022. https://www.techopedia.com/definition/4923/web-30.

12. Plavnik, Julie. "The Creator Economy: How We Arrived There, and Why We Need Its Web3 Upgrade." *Cointelegraph*, July 16, 2022. https://cointelegraph.com/news/the-creator-economy-how-we-arrived-there-and-why-we-need-its-web3-upgrade.

13. Godbout, Ted. "Wealth Transfers to Hit $84 Trillion through 2045." National Association of Plan Advisors, January 27, 2022. https://www.napa-net.org/news-info/daily-news/wealth-transfers-hit-84-trillion-through-2045.

14. Tardi, Carla. "Near Field Communication (NFC) Definition." *Investopedia*, September 23, 2020. https://www.investopedia.com/terms/n/near-field-communication-nfc.asp.

15. "What Can You Buy with Bitcoin: A Beginners Guide to Spending Your BTC." *Cointelegraph*, November 24, 2021. https://cointelegraph.com/bitcoin-for-beginners/what-can-you-buy-with-bitcoin-a-beginners-guide-to-spending-your-btc.

16. Csiszar, John. "How 2021 Changed Investing Forever." GOBankingRates, January 17, 2022. https://www.gobankingrates.com/investing/strategy/year-in-review-how-2021-changed-investing-forever/.

17. Furhmann, Ryan. "How the Internet Has Changed Investing." *Investopedia*, July 31, 2022. https://www.investopedia.com/financial-edge/0212/how-the-internet-has-changed-investing.aspx.

18. Wu, Jennifer, Michael Siegel, and Joshua Manion. "Online Trading: An Internet Revolution." Web MIT, June 1999. http://web.mit.edu/smadnick/www/home.html.

19. "The Rise of Newly Empowered Retail Investors." Deloitte United States. Accessed October 4, 2022. https://www2.deloitte.com/us/en/pages/financial-services/articles/the-future-of-retail-brokerage.html.

20. "McKinsey's Private Markets Annual Review." McKinsey & Company, March 24, 2022. https://www.mckinsey.com/industries/private-equity-and-principal-investors/our-insights/mckinseys-private-markets-annual-review.

21. "Private Markets Rally to New Heights." McKinsey & Company, March 2022. https://www.mckinsey.com/about-us/media.

22. O'Hare, Mark. "The Future of Alternatives." Preqin. Accessed October 5, 2022. https://docs.preqin.com/reports/Preqin-Future-of-Alternatives-Report-October-2018.pdf.

23. Nesbitt, Stephen. "Long-Term Private Equity Performance: 2000 to 2021: Portfolio for the Future." CAIA, July 20, 2022. https://caia.org/blog/2022/07/20/long-term-private-equity-performance-2000-2021.

24. "Free Online Calculators—Math, Fitness, Finance, Science." Calculator.net. Accessed October 4, 2022. https://www.calculator.net/investment-calculator.html?ctype=endamount&ctargetamountv=1000000&cstartingprinciplev=100000&cyearsv=10&cinterestratev=10&ccompound=annually&ccontributeamountv=0&cadditionat1=end&ciadditionat1=monthly&printit=0&x=75&y=18.

25. Nesbitt, "Long-Term Private Equity Performance: 2000 to 2021."

26. "Free Online Calculators—Math, Fitness, Finance, Science."

27. "Accredited Investor." SEC Emblem, April 28, 2022. https://www.sec.gov/education/capitalraising/building-blocks/accredited-investor.

28. Hayes, Adam. "Accredited Investor Defined: Understand the Requirements." *Investopedia*, July 12, 2022. https://www.investopedia.com/terms/a/accreditedinvestor.asp.

29. "Accredited Investor." SEC Emblem.

30. https://www.ellevest.com/about-us.

31. "Titan Announces Exclusive Partnership With Cathie Wood's ARK Invest, Democratizing Access to Venture Capital Funds for the Everyday Investor."

Business Wire, September 27, 2022. https://www.businesswire.com/news/home/20220927005065/en/Titan-Announces-Exclusive-Partnership-With-Cathie-Wood's-ARK-Invest-Democratizing-Access-to-Venture-Capital-Funds-for-the-Everyday-Investor.

32. Semenova, Alexandra. "Apollo, Carlyle Launch Funds on A16z-Backed Titan as PE's Retail Push Expands." Yahoo! Finance, September 13, 2022. https://finance.yahoo.com/news/apollo-carlyle-private-markets-retail-investors-titan-140014353.html.

33. Semenova, Alexandra. "ARK Invest Launches Private Fund for Retail Clients with A16z-Backed Titan." Yahoo! Finance, September 27, 2022. https://finance.yahoo.com/news/ark-invest-venture-fund-retail-clients-titan-app-130900829.html.

34. Capolaghi, Laurent, and Sonia Michel Sonia Michel. "The Future of Private Equity: Embracing the 'Retail Revolution'?" EY Luxembourg, March 16, 2022. https://www.ey.com/en_lu/private-equity/the-future-of-private-equity--embracing-the--retail-revolution--.

35. Benson, Alana. "Environmental, Social and Governance (ESG) Investing and How to Get Started." NerdWallet, August 18, 2022. https://www.nerdwallet.com/article/investing/esg-investing.

36. Ibid.

37. Venkataramani, Swetha. "85% of Investors Considered ESG Factors in Their Investment Propositions." Gartner, June 10, 2021. https://www.gartner.com/smarterwithgartner/the-esg-imperative-7-factors-for-finance-leaders-to-consider.

38. Bhagat, Sanjai. "An Inconvenient Truth about ESG Investing." *Harvard Business Review*, March 31, 2022. https://hbr.org/2022/03/an-inconvenient-truth-about-esg-investing.

39. Wu, Jennifer. "ESG Outlook 2022: The Future of ESG Investing." J.P. Morgan Asset Management, January 2, 2022. https://am.jpmorgan.com/dk/en/asset-management/liq/investment-themes/sustainable-investing/future-of-esg-investing/.

40. Taylor, Tania Lynn, and Sean Collins. "ESG Investing and Sustainability." Deloitte Insights. April 5, 2022. https://www2.deloitte.com/uk/en/insights/industry/financial-services/esg-investing-and-sustainability.html.

41. Iansiti, Marco, and Karim Lakhani. "The Truth about Blockchain." *Harvard Business Review,* February 2017. https://hbr.org/2017/01/the-truth-about-blockchain.

42. https://www.blockchainresearchinstitute.org/an-intro-to-blockchain-and-nfts/.

43. *Wikipedia,* s.v. "cryptography." Accessed October 9, 2022. https://en.wikipedia.org/wiki/Cryptography.

44. Bonnie. "How Does Cryptocurrency Work?" CryptoCurrency Facts, November 5, 2017. https://cryptocurrencyfacts.com/how-does-cryptocurrency-work-2/.

45. Lehnis, Marianne. "More Than a Ledger: How Blockchains Will Democratize Wealth." *Bitcoin Magazine*, July 31, 2018. https://bitcoinmagazine.com/culture/more-ledger-how-blockchains-will-democratize-wealth.

46. Sharma, Rakesh. "What Is Decentralized Finance (DeFi) and How Does It Work?" *Investopedia*, September 21, 2022. https://www.investopedia.com/decentralized-finance-defi-5113835.

47. Roose, Kevin. "What Is Defi?" *New York Times*, March 18, 2022. https://www.nytimes.com/interactive/2022/03/18/technology/what-is-defi-cryptocurrency.html.

48. "Securitize Launches Fund Providing Tokenized Exposure to KKR Fund." Securitize, September 13, 2022. https://securitize.io/press-releases/securitize-kkr-tokenized-fund.

49. "How Blockchain Tech Can Power ESG Initiatives That Really Work." *Kaleido*. Accessed October 5, 2022. https://www.kaleido.io/industries/esg.

Chapter 6

1. *Online Etymology Dictionary*, s.v. "wealth." Accessed October 5, 2022. https://www.etymonline.com/word/wealth#etymonline_v_4871.

2. *Online Etymology Dictionary*, s.v. "weal." Accessed October 5, 2022. https://www.etymonline.com/search?q=weal.

3. Woolf, Steven H., Laudan Aron, Sarah M. Simon, Emily Zimmerman, and Kim X. Lux. "How Are Income and Wealth Linked to Health and Longevity?" Society Health VCU, April 2015. https://societyhealth.vcu.edu/media/society-health/pdf/IHIBrief1.pdf.

4. Lee, Dong Hoon, Leandro F.M. Rezende, Hee-Kyung Joh, NaNa Keum, Gerson Ferrari, Juan Pablo Rey-Lopez, Eric B. Rimm, Fred K. Tabung, and Edward L. Giovannucci. "Long-Term Leisure-Time Physical Activity Intensity and All-Cause and Cause-Specific Mortality: A Prospective Cohort of US Adults." *AHA Journals,* July 25, 2022. https://www.ahajournals.org/doi/abs/10.1161/CIRCULATIONAHA.121.058162.

5. https://agentestudio.com/blog/healthcare-app-gamification.

6. "Millennials Infographic." Goldman Sachs. Accessed October 5, 2022. https://www.goldmansachs.com/insights/archive/millennials/.

7. Brennan, Dan, MD. "Mental Health: How It Affects Your Physical Health." WebMD, March 29, 2021. https://www.webmd.com/mental-health/how-does-mental-health-affect-physical-health.

8. Ohrnberger, Julius, Eleonora Fichera, and Matt Sutton. "The Relationship between Physical and Mental Health: A Mediation Analysis." *Social Science & Medicine* 195 (2017): 42–49. https://pubmed.ncbi.nlm.nih.gov/29132081/.

9. "Our History." Mental Health America. Accessed October 5, 2022. https://www.mhanational.org/our-history.

10. Maldonado, Marissa. "How Stress Affects Mental Health." Psych Central, February 25, 2014. https://psychcentral.com/blog/how-stress-affects-mental-health#1.

11. Ibid.

12. "Stress in America." Press release, American Psychological Association, March 2021. https://www.apa.org/news/press/releases/stress/.

13. Liggins, Owen. "The Stress Bucket—Managing Your Stress." Student Life. University of Lincoln, January 21, 2021. https://studentlife.lincoln.ac.uk/2021/01/21/the-stress-bucket-managing-your-stress/.

14. *Etymology Online Dictionary*, s.v. "spirit." Accessed October 5, 2022. https://www.etymonline.com/word/spirit?ref=etymonline_crossreference#etymonline_v_24031.

15. Ghaderi, Ahmad, Seyed Mahmoud Tabatabaei, Saharnaz Nedjat, Mohsen Javadi, and Bagher Larijani. "Explanatory Definition of the Concept of Spiritual Health: A Qualitative Study in Iran." *Journal of Medical Ethics and History of Medicine*. Tehran University of Medical Sciences, April 9, 2018. https://www.ncbi.nlm.nih.gov/pmc/articles/PMC6150917/.

16. Helmer, Jodi. "What Happens to Your Brain on Psychedelics? Experts Explain the Benefits and Risks." *Fortune*, September 27, 2022. https://fortune.com/well/2022/09/27/psychedelics-benefits-and-risks/.

17. Beres, Derek. "How Psychedelics Helped Shape Modern Technology." *Psychedelic Spotlight*, January 19, 2021. https://psychedelicspotlight.com/how-psychedelics-shaped-modern-technology/.

18. *Wikipedia*, s.v. "psychedelic therapy." https://en.wikipedia.org/wiki/Psychedelic_therapy.

19. "Sex, Drugs and Aldous Huxley." Dangerous Visions series. BBC. https://www.bbc.co.uk/programmes/articles/4TQhTRDcHw1V0YhbtL600BJ/sex-drugs-and-aldous-huxley.

20. *Wikipedia*, s.v. "psychedelic therapy." https://en.wikipedia.org/wiki/Psychedelic_therapy.

21. Beres, "How Psychedelics Helped Shape Modern Technology."

22. "Psychedelic Drugs: A Market Poised for Takeoff." KPMG, June 2022. https://advisory.kpmg.us/content/dam/advisory/en/pdfs/2022/psychedelic-drugs-market-poised-for-takeoff.pdf.

23. Callaghan, Shaun, Martin Lösch, Anna Pione, and Warren Teichner. "Feeling Good: The Future of the $1.5 Trillion Wellness Market." McKinsey & Company, April 8, 2021. https://www.mckinsey.com/industries/consumer-packaged-goods/our-insights/feeling-good-the-future-of-the-1-5-trillion-wellness-market.

24. *Online Etymology Dictionary*, s.v. "play (v.)." Accessed October 5, 2022. https://www.etymonline.com/search?q=play.

25. Porter, Scott, John Harrison, Adrian Ang, Rich Golik, and Sandeep Gupta. "What's Possible for the Gaming Industry in the next Dimension?" Ernst & Young. Accessed October 5, 2022. https://www.ey.com/en_us/tmt/what-s-possible-for-the-gaming-industry-in-the-next-dimension?WT.mc_id=10819252&AA.tsrc=paidsearch&gclid=Cj0KCQjwmdGYBhDRARIsABmSEePvKD_ieJ0nFWt652q6zeKRp1Zu2OWR0EpuKV-PApcvnFqRSW-WLRMaArgUEALw_wcB.

26. Ibid.

Chapter 7

1. "10 Critical Difference between Information and Knowledge with Table." Core Differences. Accessed October 5, 2022. https://coredifferences.com/difference-between-information-and-knowledge/.

2. Varghese, T. K. (2020). Building Multidisciplinary Teams in the Digital Age. In T. Wang and A. Beck, (eds.), *Building a Clinical Practice. Success in Academic Surgery*. Cham: Springer. https://doi.org/10.1007/978-3-030-29271-3_4

3. Schilling, David Russell. "Knowledge Doubling Every 12 Months, Soon to Be Every 12 Hours." *Industry Tap*, April 19, 2013. https://www.industrytap.com/knowledge-doubling-every-12-months-soon-to-be-every-12-hours/3950.

4. Chamberlain, Paul. "Knowledge Is Not Everything." *Design For Health* 4, no. 1 (February 13, 2020): 1–3. https://doi.org/10.1080/24735132.2020.1731203.

5. "10 Critical Difference between Information and Knowledge with Table."

6. "The Rise of Newly Empowered Retail Investors." Deloitte. Accessed October 5, 2022. https://www2.deloitte.com/us/en/pages/financial-services/articles/the-future-of-retail-brokerage.html.

7. Aparicio, G., T. Iturralde, and A. V. Rodríguez. "Developments in the Knowledge-Based Economy Research Field: A Bibliometric Literature Review." *Management Review Quarterly* (2021). https://doi.org/10.1007/s11301-021-00241-w

8. Ibid.

9. Spacey, John. "11 Examples of the Knowledge Economy." Simplicable, January 24, 2018. https://simplicable.com/new/knowledge-economy.

10. Seidman, Dov. "From the Knowledge Economy to the Human Economy." *Harvard Business Review*, November 12, 2014. https://hbr.org/2014/11/from-the-knowledge-economy-to-the-human-economy.

11. Aparicio, Iturralde, and Rodríguez, "Developments in the Knowledge-Based Economy Research Field."

12. "U.S. Small Business Administration Frequently Asked Questions." U.S. Small Business Administration Office of Advocacy, December 2021. https://cdn.advocacy.sba.gov/wp-content/uploads/2021/12/06095731/Small-Business-FAQ-Revised-December-2021.pdf.

13. Nielson, Laura. "Welcome to the Golden Age of the Private Club." *Wall Street Journal*, August 12, 2022. https://www.wsj.com/articles/inside-new-guard-golden-age-private-social-clubs-members-only-11660306883.

14. Ibid.

15. Ibid.

16. Blumberg, Paul. "The Decline and Fall of the Status Symbol: Some Thoughts on Status in a Post-Industrial Society." *Social Problems* 21, no. 4 (1974): 480–498. https://doi.org/10.2307/799987.

17. *Wikipedia*, s.v. "Tyrian purple." Accessed October 5, 2022. https://en.wikipedia.org/wiki/Tyrian_purple.

18. *Cambridge English Dictionary Online*, s.v. "influence." Accessed October 5, 2022. https://dictionary.cambridge.org/us/dictionary/english/influence.

19. Peters, Tom. "The Brand Called You." *Fast Company*, August 31, 1997. https://www.fastcompany.com/28905/brand-called-you.

20. "The Business of Influencing Is Not Frivolous. It's Serious." *The Economist*, April 2, 2022. https://www.economist.com/business/2022/04/02/the-business-of-influencing-is-not-frivolous-its-serious .

21. Droesch, Blake. "Influencers More Likely to Inspire Gen Zer and Millennial Purchases." *Insider Intelligence*, February 13, 2020. https://www.insiderintelligence.com/content/influencers-more-likely-to-inspire-gen-zer-and-millennial-purchases.

22. *Wikipedia*, s.v. "Morning Consult." Accessed October 6, 2022. https://en.wikipedia.org/wiki/Morning_Consult.

23. *Wikipedia*, s.v. "How to Win Friends and Influence People." Accessed October 6, 2022. https://en.wikipedia.org/wiki/How_to_Win_Friends_and_Influence_People.

24. Santora, Jacinda. "Key Influencer Marketing Statistics You Need to Know for 2022." *Influencer Marketing Hub*, August 3, 2022. https://influencermarketinghub.com/influencer-marketing-statistics/.

25. Ibid.

Chapter 8

1. *Wikipedia*, s.v. "time." Accessed October 6, 2022. https://en.wikipedia.org/wiki/Time.

2. Heyford, Shauna Carther. "Understanding the Time Value of Money." *Investopedia*, May 23, 2022. https://www.investopedia.com/articles/03/082703.asp.

3. AHEC. "How Much Is Your Time Really Worth? Time vs Money Dilemma." *AHEConline Blog*, June 3, 2019. https://aheconline.blog/2019/06/03/how-much-is-your-time-really-worth-time-vs-money-dilemma/.

4. *Wikipedia*, s.v. "refrigerator." Accessed October 6, 2022. https://en.wikipedia.org/wiki/Refrigerator#:˜:text=The%20first%20cooling%20systems%20for, machine%20was%20invented%20in%201854.

5. "What Is Energy?" U.S. Energy Information Administration (EIA), December 13, 2021. https://www.eia.gov/energyexplained/what-is-energy/.

6. Schwartz, Tony, and Catherine McCarthy. "Manage Your Energy, Not Your Time." *Harvard Business Review,* 2007. https://hbr.org/2007/10/manage-your-energy-not-your-time?registration=success.

7. "What Is Energy?"

8. "Ibid.

9. Kane, Lexie. "The Attention Economy." Nielsen Norman Group, June 30, 2019. https://www.nngroup.com/articles/attention-economy/.

10. Howarth, Josh. "Time Spent Using Smartphones (2022 Statistics)." *Exploding Topics*, September 16, 2022. https://explodingtopics.com/blog/smartphone-usage-stats.

11. Stephanie. "Pareto Distribution Definition." *Statistics How To*, October 12, 2017. https://www.statisticshowto.com/pareto-distribution/.

12. Kos, Blaz. "The Pareto Principle (the 80:20 Rule) in Time Management." *Spica*, December 23, 2020. https://www.spica.com/blog/the-pareto-principle-in-time-management.

13. Kane, Lexie. "The Attention Economy." Nielsen Norman Group, June 30, 2019. https://www.nngroup.com/articles/attention-economy/.

14. Ibid.

15. Patel, Lomit. "The Attention Economy Is Worth Billions of Dollars." *HackerNoon*, July 24, 2022. https://hackernoon.com/the-attention-economy-is-worth-billions-of-dollars.

16. Kish, Leonard. "Web3 And Shifts in the Attention Economy." *VentureBeat*, August 6, 2022. https://venturebeat.com/datadecisionmakers/web3-and-shifts-in-the-attention-economy/.

17. *Merriam-Webster Online Dictionary*, s.v. "experience." Accessed October 6, 2022. https://www.merriam-webster.com/dictionary/experience.

18. Hoffower, Hillary. "The Elite's Favorite Status Symbols Have Become Way More Expensive over the Past 20 Years." *Business Insider India*, March 4, 2021. https://www.businessinsider.in/policy/economy/news/the-elites-favorite-status-symbols-have-become-way-more-expensive-over-the-past-20-years/articleshow/81181265.cms?module=inline&pgtype=article.

19. Buchanan, Greg, and Joe Kruger. "Experiences Will Be Top of Mind for Consumers in 2022." Microsoft Advertising, March 24, 2022. https://about.ads.microsoft.com/en-us/blog/post/march-2022/experiences-will-be-top-of-mind-for-consumers-in-2022.

20. Roches, Les. "What Is the Experience Economy?" *Insights*, August 8, 2022. https://insights.ehotelier.com/insights/2022/08/08/what-is-the-experience-economy/.

21. Goldman, Dan, Sophie Marchessou, and Warren Teichner. "Cashing in on the US Experience Economy." McKinsey & Company, September 16, 2020. https://www.mckinsey.com/industries/private-equity-and-principal-investors/our-insights/cashing-in-on-the-us-experience-economy.

22. Landau, Elizabeth. "Study: Experiences Make Us Happier Than Possessions." CNN. Accessed October 6, 2022. https://www.cnn.com/2009/HEALTH/02/10/happiness.possessions/.

23. Levine, Saul. "A Sense of Awe, and 'Peak Experiences,'" *Psychology Today*, May 5, 2021. https://www.psychologytoday.com/us/blog/our-emotional-footprint/202105/sense-awe-and-peak-experiences.

24. "StoryTech at CES." PCBC, 2019. https://www.pcbc.com/PCBC/CUSTOM/Exhibits/StoryTechTrendsSample.pdf.

25. Gherini, Anne. "Millennials Ignited the Experience Economy, Here Is How to Cash In." *Inc.*, October 31, 2018. https://www.inc.com/anne-gherini/cash-in-on-experience-economy.html.

26. *Wikipedia*, s.v. "meta." Accessed October 6, 2022. https://en.wikipedia.org/wiki/Meta.

27. Reaume, Amanda. "The Metaverse? What It Is & What You Should Know." *Seeking Alpha*, June 16, 2022. https://seekingalpha.com/article/4472812-what-is-metaverse.

Chapter 9

1. Daniel Jones. "The 36 Questions That Lead to Love." *New York Times*, January 9, 2015. https://www.nytimes.com/2015/01/09/style/no-37-big-wedding-or-small.html.

2. Arthur Aron et al. "The Experimental Generation of Interpersonal Closeness: A Procedure and Some Preliminary Findings." *Personality and Social Psychology Bulletin* 23, no. 4 (1997): 363–377. https://doi.org/10.1177/0146167297234003.

3. Wines, Jennifer. "Council Post: The Power of Voice in Business: Insights from Silicon Valley's Newest Voice-Based Social Media App." *Forbes*, December 14, 2020. https://www.forbes.com/sites/forbesbusinessdevelopmentcouncil/2020/12/15/the-power-of-voice-in-business-insights-from-silicon-valleys-newest-voice-based-social-media-app/?sh=30f526bc453a.

4. Boutet, Isabelle, Megan LeBlanc, Justin A. Chamberland, and Charles A. Collin. "Emojis Influence Emotional Communication, Social Attributions, and Information Processing." *Computers in Human Behavior* 119 (June 2021): 106722. https://doi.org/10.1016/j.chb.2021.106722.

5. Goeke, Niklas. "The Speed of Trust Summary." Four Minute Books, February 10, 2016. https://fourminutebooks.com/the-speed-of-trust-summary/.

6. Kaufman, David. "For Elite? Yes. Ostentatious? Yes. But Also Effective." *New York Times,* May 21, 2022. https://www.nytimes.com/2022/05/21/business/world-economic-forum-davos-accomplish.html.

7. Wines, "Council Post."

8. Barroso, Amanda, Kim Parker, and Jesse Bennett. "As Millennials near 40, They're Approaching Family Life Differently Than Previous Generations." Pew Research Center, May 27, 2020. https://www.pewresearch.org/social-trends/2020/05/27/as-millennials-near-40-theyre-approaching-family-life-differently-than-previous-generations/.

9. Cachero, Paulina, and Ella Ceron. "Why Aren't Millennials Buying Home? 4 Charts Explain." Bloomberg, March 23, 2022. https://www.bloomberg.com/news/articles/2022-03-23/why-aren-t-millennials-buying-home-4-charts-explain#xj4y7vzkg.

10. Barroso, Parker, and Bennett. "As Millennials near 40."

11. Meyers, Alyssa. "Spurred on by Covid-19, Millennials Lead the Way in Destigmatizing Online Dating." *Morning Consult*, February 11, 2021. https://morningconsult.com/2021/02/11/online-dating-stigma-amid-pandemic/.

12. Ibid.

13. Ibid.

14. Curry, David. "Dating App Revenue and Usage Statistics (2022)." Business of Apps, August 31, 2022. https://www.businessofapps.com/data/dating-app-market/~:text=Tinder%20is%20the%20leader%20in,share%20every%20year%20since%202017.

15. Schwartz, Barry. *The Paradox of Choice*. The Decision Lab. Accessed September 22, 2022. https://thedecisionlab.com/reference-guide/economics/the-paradox-of-choice.

16. Ibid.

17. Nicholson, Jeremy. "What Jordan Peterson Gets Right about Relationships." *Psychology Today*, September 24, 2021. https://www.psychology today.com/us/blog/the-attraction-doctor/202109/what-jordan-peterson-gets-right-about-relationships.

18. Everitt, Lauren. "Ten Key Moments in the History of Marriage." BBC News, March 14, 2012. https://www.bbc.com/news/magazine-17351133.

19. Ibid.

20. Ibid.

21. Ibid.

22. Ibid.

23. *Merriam-Webster Online*, s.v. "sacrament." Accessed September 23, 2022. https://www.merriam-webster.com/dictionary/sacrament~:text=Definition%20of%20 sacrament,comparable%20to%20a%20Christian%20sacrament.

24. Everitt, "Ten Key Moments in the History of Marriage."

25. Adamy, Janet. "U.S. Marriage Rate Plunges to Lowest Level on Record." *Wall Street Journal*, April 29, 2020. https://www.wsj.com/articles/u-s-marriage-rate-plunges-to-lowest-level-on-record-11588132860.

26. Ibid.

27. Ibid.

28. Cherry, Kendra. "How Do Individualistic Cultures Influence Behavior?" Verywell Mind, December 11, 2020. https://www.verywellmind.com/what-are-individualistic-cultures-2795273.

29. Forsberg, Edit. "Marriage and Individualism—Is There a Connection?" Stockholm University, 2020. https://www.diva-portal.org/smash/get/diva2:1485242/FULLTEXT01.pdf.

Chapter 10

1. "The Difference between Principles and Values." *Plan Plus Online*, January 11, 2019. https://www.planplusonline.com/difference-principles-values/.

2. "The Difference between Principles and Values."

3. Hoomans, Dr. Joel. "35,000 Decisions: The Great Choices of Strategic Leaders." The Learning Edge. Roberts Wesleyan College, March 20, 2015. https://go.roberts.edu/leadingedge/the-great-choices-of-strategic-leaders.

4. Xiao, Wen S. "The Role of Collectivism—Individualism in Attitudes toward Compliance and Psychological Responses during the Covid-19 Pandemic." *Frontiers in Psychology* 12 (October 28, 2021). https://doi.org/10.3389/fpsyg.2021.600826.

5. Nickerson, Charlotte. "Individualistic Cultures and Behavior." *Simply Psychology*, September 22, 2021. https://www.simplypsychology.org/what-are-individualistic-cultures.html.

6. "Making Sense of Cross-Cultural Communication." Clearly Cultural. Accessed September 26, 2022. https://clearlycultural.com/geert-hofstede-cultural-dimensions/individualism/.

7. Ibid.

8. "Country Comparison." *Hofstede Insights*, June 21, 2021. https://www.hofstede-insights.com/country-comparison/canada,japan,the-usa/.

9. Clear, James. "Core Values List." *James Clear* (blog), June 12, 2018. https://jamesclear.com/core-values.

Chapter 11

1. Gabriel, Angeli. "How 'Captain Planet' Inspired an Environmental Movement." Fox Weather, April 22, 2022. https://www.foxweather.com/lifestyle/captain-planet-and-the-planeteers-show-history.

2. Dhir, Rajeev. "Nonrenewable Resources Definition." *Investopedia*, May 27, 2022. https://www.investopedia.com/terms/n/nonrenewableresource.asp.

3. Dhir, "Nonrenewable Resources Definition."

4. Ibid.

5. "What Is Energy?" U.S. Energy Information Administration (EIA), June 28, 2022. https://www.eia.gov/energyexplained/what-is-energy/sources-of-energy.php.

6. "U.S. Energy Facts Explained." U.S. Energy Information Administration (EIA), April 2022. https://www.eia.gov/energyexplained/us-energy-facts/.

7. Ibid.

About the Author

Born in Mexico to an Irish mother and Mexican father, Jennifer moved ten times by the age of twenty, all over North America. After law school, she embarked on a career in private wealth management, which immersed her into the world of immense wealth.

Jennifer worked at some of the top private wealth management institutes in the world, namely Goldman Sachs, JPMorgan, and Fidelity. She earned her Juris Doctor from Suffolk University Law School in Boston, and her Certified Private Wealth Advisor designation from Booth Business School in Chicago. While at Fidelity, she developed a proof of concept and prototype for an enterprise solution, which was advanced into incubation.

Her strong background with words (law) and numbers (finance), paired with her entrepreneurial spirit, make her a trusted voice on the topic of *redefining wealth* for the *new wealth paradigm*.

Recently named one of the Top 100 Women of the Future, Jennifer is a certified private wealth advisor who founded Invisible Wealth, which provides strategic, future-forward, advisory services.

> *"Vision is the art of seeing what is invisible to others."*
> —*Jonathan Swift*

Index